The Productive Retirement Years of Former Managers

THE CONFERENCE BOARD

THE CONFERENCE BOARD is an independent, nonprofit business research organization. For more than sixty years it has continuously served as an institution for scientific research in the fields of business economics and business management. Its sole purpose is to promote prosperity and security by assisting in the effective operation and sound development of voluntary productive enterprise.

The Board has more than 4,000 Associates and serves 40,000 individuals throughout the world. It does continuing research in the fields of economic conditions, marketing, finance, personnel administration, international activities, public affairs, antitrust, and various other related areas.

Associates may consult the Board and its research staff for additional information on this report or any other management subject.

For information concerning membership in The Conference Board and its services and facilities, contact the Associate Relations Division.

©1978 THE CONFERENCE BOARD, INC.
845 Third Avenue, New York, N.Y. 10022

THE CONFERENCE BOARD IN CANADA
25 McArthur Road, Ottawa, Ontario, K1L-6R3, Canada

THE CONFERENCE BOARD IN EUROPE
Avenue Louise 149, 1050 Brussels, Belgium

Prices: $ 5.00—Associate
       $15.00—Non-Associate

   For prices on orders for classroom use, contact the Information Service Division.

Conference Board Report No. 747   Printed in U.S.A.

Library of Congress Catalog No.: 78-58831
ISBN No.: 0-8237-0180-8

The Productive Retirement Years of Former Managers

Walter S. Wikstrom

*A Research Report from The Conference Board's
Division of Management Research
Harold Stieglitz, Vice President*

About This Report

This report is concerned with the post-retirement activities of a very select part of the older population of the United States—persons who occupied positions in middle and top management of major U.S. firms at the time they retired. The report focuses especially on their continued involvement with work, both income- producing and volunteer, but it also deals with other activities in which they engage, such as sports and hobbies. Where meaningful, the report relates current activities to former occupational roles.

Two-thirds of the respondents have been engaged in work—for income or as volunteers—at some time since they retired and over half are currently working. Of those who are working now, 56 percent derive income from their work, while 66 percent engage in volunteer work. The figures add to more than 100 percent because almost a quarter are engaged in both types of activity.

Indeed, almost one in five of the survey respondents denies that he or she is retired, instead claiming to be "as busy as ever" with paid or volunteer work—and 98 percent of them add "and I like it that way."

Those who are working are, for the most part, engaged in work similar to that which they had done in their preretirement careers. Former loan officers in banks serve part-time on loan committees, either with their former employer or with a new bank. Former production managers act as consultants on production problems. Former corporate officers serve on the board of one or more companies. A significant minority, however, have found postretirement work that is completely different from their earlier careers. A former middle manager drives a truck, and says that he thoroughly enjoys the work. Several former chief executives are busy running cattle ranches. A former head of research and development says of his second career as a professor of engineering that "it is the realization of a lifelong ambition."

Similarly, while some retirees engaged in volunteer work different from any work they had done in their preretirement careers, most who have volunteered do work similar to what they have done before. They serve on boards and advisory committees; they keep books or manage investment portfolios for voluntary agencies; they supervise the maintenance of churches or community centers. In fact, many had done similar work *as volunteers* before retiring; about two-thirds of the postretirement volunteers had been volunteers prior to retiring and, of those, three-quarters did substantially similar work in the two periods.

The higher in the corporate hierarchy the retiree had been before retiring, the greater is the probability that he or she will continue to work after retiring, either for pay or as a volunteer. Former chief executives and corporate officers are overrepresented among the retiree-workers; former middle managers are underrepresented. And former bankers are overrepresented among both the paid and volunteer workers in retirement.

The retirees are active in other ways. Three-quarters engage in active sports. More than four out of five regularly pursue hobbies and travel for pleasure. While there is some decline in these activities with advancing age, even among the oldest retirees—those 77 years of age or older—over half regularly engage in active sports and about three-quarters pursue hobbies and travel.

Indeed, to keep active is the advice that the retirees would give to other persons who want a happy retirement. Any activities one enjoys are acceptable for some of the respondents. For others, however, postretirement activities must be "meaningful." "Meaningful activity" translates into work for which one is paid, for some of the retirees, while for others it means voluntary work that is of service to others and to the community at large.

Inflation—and the fear of continued inflation—is the major concern expressed by these former managers. Worries about the erosion of purchasing power of their retirement incomes is expressed not only by the relatively few whose annual funds are $7,000 or less but also by those who have $60,000 or more to spend annually—and by all groups in between.

On the whole, however, these retirees are very happy. On a standardized "Satisfaction with Life" scale, on which scores can range from a low of 0 to a high of 36, the median score for these former managers and professionals is 30. When asked to suggest what might improve the quality of their retirement lives, many say simply: "I'm happy as I am."

These former managers and professionals were overwhelmingly responsive to the survey on which this report is based. They seem eager to provide information about themselves, and many say that they are grateful that their former employers and The Conference Board are interested in their experiences. Replies were received from over 3,800 retirees, about two-thirds of the survey sample.

The exact response rate can not be determined because of the procedure followed in distributing most of the questionnaires. Cooperating companies agreed to select retirees to be included in the sample according to criteria that were designed to yield a representative sample of upper-level managers who had retired between 1961 and 1976. About a third of the firms supplied mailing lists to the Board on the understanding that the lists would be destroyed after envelopes were typed. Two-thirds of the firms followed a method that they and the Board considered preferable, giving even greater assurance of anonymity to the retirees. Supplies of up to 30 survey packets were sent in bulk to these companies, which added the names and addresses of their retirees and remailed them. In that way the Board never knew the identity of the retirees in the sample, while the cooperating companies have never seen the responses.

However, it is known that many firms discovered that they had overestimated the number of retirees who might meet the selection criteria. Not all the questionnaires sent to these companies were, in fact, remailed; the exact number is unknown. If all had been, the response rate would be a high 59 percent. It is estimated that 80 percent were mailed to retirees, yielding a response rate of 69 percent, exceptionally high for a mail survey.

ABOUT THIS REPORT

Contents

	Page
ABOUT THIS REPORT	ii
FOREWORD	vii

1. OVERVIEW 1
   The Age of the Respondents 2
   Mandatory Retirement, Inflation and the Ages at
      which Employees Retire 4

2. INCOME-PRODUCING WORK 8
   What Do They Do? 8
      One's Own Retirement Business 10
   Age and the Prevalence of Paid Work 10
   Time Spent in Income-Producing Work 12
   Similarity of Current and Former Work 13
   Satisfactions and Dissatisfactions 13
   Finding Work 14
   Interest in Paid Work on the Part of Nonworking Retirees 15

3. SERVING OTHERS THROUGH VOLUNTARY WORK 18
   What Do They Do? 18
   Volunteering Began Before Retirement 19
   Which Retirees Volunteer? 21
   Time Spent at Volunteer Work 22
   Satisfactions and Dissatisfactions 23
   How Were They Recruited? 25

4. AVOCATIONS 28
   Sports 28
   Hobbies 29
   Formal Education 30
   Travel 31
   How Time Was Spent "Yesterday" 31

	Page
5. THE QUALITY OF LIFE	33
The Highly Satisfied and the Least	35
"Satisfaction" or "Optimism"	35
Improving the Quality of Retirement Life	36
Suggestions for Others like Oneself	37
"Working" and "Nonworking" Retirees Compared	38
APPENDIX	40
About the Retirees	40
The Former Work of the Retirees	40
Current Income	41
Health and Physical Condition	44
Residence	44

Tables

	Page
1. Demographic Data on Retirees and Comparisons with the Population at Large	3
2. Age Distribution of Respondents	4
3. Current Status and Retirees' Reactions to It	4
4. Age of Retirees at Retirement	5
5. Changes in Age at Retirement in Recent Years	5
6. Extent of Income-Producing Work during Retirement	9
7. Satisfactions Gained from Income-Producing Work	14
8. Dissatisfactions Associated with Income-Producing Work	14
9. Retirees' Sources of Leads to Employment	15
10. Interest in Income-Producing Work Reported by Retirees Not Now Working	16
11. When and How Required Knowledge and Skills were Obtained	16
12. Volunteer Work Before and After Retirement Compared	21
13. Satisfactions Gained from Volunteer Work	24
14. Dissatisfactions Associated with Volunteer Work	24
15. How Retirees Were Recruited for Volunteer Work	25

		Page
16.	Interest in Volunteer Work Reported by Retirees Not Now Involved	25
17.	When and How Required Knowledge and Skills were Obtained	26
18.	Participation in Active Sports	28
19.	Participation in Avocational Activities, by Age of Retirees	29
20.	Pursuit of Hobbies	29
21.	Formal Study by Retirees	30
22.	Recreational Travel	31
23.	"Satisfaction with Life" of the Retirees and the Public Aged 65 and Over	34
24.	Industries in which Retirees Formerly Worked	41
25.	Type of Former Position	41
26.	Former Functional Area of Management	41
27.	Annual Family Income After Taxes	42
28.	Sources of Current Spendable Funds	43
29.	Physical Condition during Three Months Prior to Survey	44
30.	Residential Movement Since Retirement	45
31.	Urban or Rural Residence	45

Charts

1.	Percent of Retirees Engaged in Income-Producing Work, by Age	11
2.	Extent of Volunteer Work	19
3.	Time Spent by Retirees "Yesterday" at Various Common Activities	32
4.	Number of Organizations During Career and Duration of Employment with Final Organization	42
5.	Current Health and Physical Condition Compared with that in the Past	43

Exhibits

1.	Patterns of Working Time	12
2.	Patterns of Time Spent in Volunteer Work	23

Foreword

IN OUR youth-oriented society, relatively little attention has been paid to the experiences of the older population. Folklore and myths about older persons abound, much of it consisting of half-truths at best. In recent years, efforts have been made to correct the misinformation by collecting and publicizing accurate accounts of the lives of older persons, but more needs to be done. Not only is the over-65 group a growing segment of the population, but it is also one into which almost everyone will eventually grow.

One part of the myth that is still widely accepted concerns the abilities of older persons—or, rather, their lack of ability. Bluntly, it is widely believed that older persons just are not very good at getting things done. Exceptions are considered merely to "prove the rule." It was primarily to test this myth that The Conference Board undertook this study: For if older persons are, in fact, more capable than is generally assumed, then this growing part of the population represents a national resource that is being overlooked as we consider ways of dealing with the nation's problems.

The results of the study, documented in this report, refute the myth. Not only are older persons still capable of "getting things done," they are already engaged in doing a great many things useful to themselves and to the communities in which they live.

As with all studies undertaken by the Board, the cooperation of a great many individuals and organizations was necessary to the success of this effort. The Board acknowledges its gratitude to all of them. The Edna McConnell Clark Foundation provided a generous grant to underwrite the major expenses of the study. Executives of 234 companies made the study possible by selecting, according to criteria established by the Board, the representative sample of middle- and top-level managers, retired up to 15 years, who would be included in the survey. However, it is to those retirees—3,820 former managers and professionals—that we are most indebted. Without their willingness to answer the voluminous questionnaire completely and thoughtfully the study would have been meaningless, if not impossible.

KENNETH A. RANDALL
President

Chapter 1
Overview

GROWING OLDER IS not an experience to which most Americans look forward with eager anticipation. Old age has had a bad press in this country. Indeed, the years beyond 60 are considered to be the worst part of adult life by the majority of the public, according to a national survey conducted in 1974 for the National Council on the Aging.[1] It is thought to be a time of loneliness, inactivity, and poor health. While two-thirds of the public said that older persons are "very wise from experience"; only a third said that they were also "very good at getting things done"; three-quarters considered them "very warm and friendly"; but less than a third thought them to be "very bright and alert." The survey revealed that older persons shared this view of themselves as a group, although most reported that they themselves were not lonely, inactive or in poor health.

In 1976, The Conference Board conducted a survey of a specialized segment of the older population—persons who had retired from middle and top management and professional positions in major United States companies in the last 15 years. The response from *these* older persons was overwhelming—3,820 (69 percent) replied—and their replies are reassuring. The vast majority are quite active and they are enjoying themselves. Over nine in ten say that they like their current status, whether that status is "completely retired," "as busy as ever with paid work, volunteer work, or both"; or "partially retired; doing a little paid or volunteer work." Whatever status they report, most of these retirees are employed, working as volunteers, or active in sports, hobbies and travel. Indeed, the advice the majority give concerning how to have a successful retirement is "Keep involved with other people and do something you enjoy."

Half of these "retirees" are working: 22 percent work as volunteers in religious, social or charitable organizations; 16 percent work for pay in some capacity; another 11 percent are busy at both paid and volunteer work. An additional 17 percent of the retirees, while not working at the time of the survey, had worked (for pay or as volunteers) at some time following their retirement from a major U.S. firm. Thus, two-thirds of the former managers or professional personnel continued to make a contribution to the country and to themselves after they had "retired." While many are not working full time, almost one in five denies being retired, claiming to be "as busy as ever" with paid or volunteer work, although at some point all "had retired" from a firm that had employed them for most of their working lives.

They are remarkably satisfied with their lives. As part of the survey, they responded to a widely used "Satisfaction With Life" scale on which

---

[1] Louis Harris and Associates, Inc., *The Myth and Reality of Aging in America,* Washington, D.C.: The National Council on the Aging, Inc., 1975.

scores can range from a depressing 0 to a euphoric 36. Half have scores of 30 or above, and only 10 percent have scores of 21 or below. A healthy vanity contributes to their satisfaction: 91 percent agree with the statement from the scale that "Compared to other people my age, I make a good appearance"—and only 1 percent completely disagree.

There is an obvious discrepancy between the popular perception of the later years of life and the experiences of these people who are living through those years. In part this is because the popular perception is at variance with the facts of later life, as the survey for the National Council on the Aging revealed. Older persons are more capable, healthier and happier than is generally assumed; while many report having problems with specific aspects of life in the United States today, the lives of most older persons are not as bleak as is commonly supposed.

However, a large part of the discrepancy stems from the fact that the participants in the Conference Board survey are a highly select part of the older population. Table 1 (p. 3) reveals some of the differences between this sample and the older population in general. The respondents to the Board's survey are almost exclusively male, although men are only 41 percent of the population of the United States aged 65 and older. It can be presumed that almost all the respondents are white, although blacks and other minorities account for 9 percent of the older population. Few women or members of minority groups occupied higher management positions at the time the "retiree" sample retired.

Over nine in ten of the respondents are married and living with their wives. That is true of only three-quarters of the men and only about a third of the women in the country 65 and older; half the older women of the country are widows. Less than 1 percent of the respondents have wives confined to nursing homes or living apart from their husbands for other reasons.

Perhaps more significant differences between the respondents and the population in general are the greater income and the higher level of education of the former. While the median before-tax income of the population 65 and older was about $7,000 in 1975, the median for the "retiree" group (in 1976) was $20,600 after taxes. Indeed, while half the "retirees" have income of $20,000 and over (after taxes), less than one in ten of the older population in general enjoys such an annual income.

As would be expected, the respondents are also well educated. About a half of the "retirees" have at least bachelors degrees. In comparison, only about a third of the population 65 and older are high school graduates; half have had one year of high school or less.

The characteristics that most sets the respondents apart from the older population of the country are their present or former occupations. All either are or have been managerial or professional employees of major United States business firms, occupying positions in the upper half of the management hierarchy. They are accustomed to planning courses of action to reach objectives and to carrying out those plans successfully. Most have decided, either before or after "retiring," what they wanted to do with their lives and, for the most part, they have been able to carry out those plans. They are, in a sense, still managing.

The Ages of the Respondents

Thus far, comparisons have been made with the total population of the United States aged 65 and older, with some being very much older. Similar comparisons with the ages of the respondents would not be meaningful because the survey group was artificially restricted in its age range. The firms that selected retirees for the study were asked to mail the Board's questionnaire only to persons who had retired from middle-management or higher positions within the 15 years prior to 1976. Inasmuch as most persons retire between the ages of 60 and 65, no very old persons are included in the group. The youngest "retiree" was 50 in 1976; the oldest was only 86. The age distribution of the respondents is given in Table 2 on page 4.

Table 1: Demographic Data on Retirees and Comparisons with the Population at Large

	Retirees	Population 65 Years and Older[1]	
Total Sample	3,679	22,400,000	
Sex	Percent[2]	Percent[2]	
Male	99	40.8	
Female	1	59.2	
Race			
White	(Note 3)	91.5[a]	
Black and other races		8.5	
Marital Status		Male	Female
Single	2	4.7	5.8
Married, living with spouse	92	77.3	37.6
Married, spouse absent	1	2.0	1.5
Widowed	5	13.6	52.5
Divorced	1	2.5	2.6
Other	b	—	—
Geographical Distributions			
Northeast	24	24.8	
Great Lakes	22	18.2	
North central	6	9.1	
Northwest	3	3.6	
Southeast	21	21.4	
South central	7	11.0	
Southwest	16	11.7	
Alaska	0	c	
Hawaii	1	.3	
Annual Family Income (After Taxes)		*"Total Money Income"—(Before Taxes)*[4]	
Median Income	$20,600	$7,298	
Under $4,000	b	Less than $2,500	8.
$ 4,000— 6,999	1	$ 2,500— 4,999	18.
7,000— 9,000	7	5,000— 7,499	20.
		7,500— 9,999	17.
10,000—14,999	19	10,000—14,999	20.
15,000—19,999	20	15,000—19,999	9.
20,000—24,999	16	20,000 and over	9.
25,000—29,999	11		
30,000—34,999	8		
35,000—39,999	5		
40,000—49,999	6		
50,000—59,999	3		
60,000 and over	5		
Educational Attainment			
Some high school but not completed	8	Median school years completed: 9 years	
High school graduate	16	Percent high school graduates: 35.2%	
Some college but not completed	24		
College graduate	32		
Additional post-graduate work in university	9		
Advance degree received	9		
Noncollegiate technical or vocational training	1		
Other	1		

[1]Unless otherwise noted, the data presented are for the population 65 years of age and older in 1975 and are based upon data reported in *Demogrpahic Aspects of Aging and the Older Population in the United States,* Current Population Reports, Series P-23, No. 59; Bureau of the Census, U.S. Department of Commerce.

[2]Percentages may not add to 100 percent because of rounding.

[3]The Conference Board questionnaire did not ask for the race of the respondent. It can be assumed that the respondents are almost 100 percent white inasmuch as few members of minority groups occupied positions at middle management or higher in major firms in the period 1961—1976 when the respondents retired from such positions.

[4]The median income figure is reported for 1974 in the Census report cited in Note 1. The detailed breakdown of annual family income is based upon 1972 data reported in Alan Fox's "Work Status and Income Change 1968-1972: Retirement History Study Review," *Social Security Bulletin,* December, 1976.

[a]These figures are based upon 1970 data, reported in the Census report cited in Note 1.
[b]Less than 0.5 percent.
[c]Less than 0.05 percent.

Table 2: Age Distribution of the Respondents

Age	Percent[1]
61 and younger	6%
62-64	11
65-66	15
67-68	18
69-70	14
71-73	16
74-76	11
77 and older	10

[1] Percentages do not add to 100 because of rounding.

A relatively small number of the "retirees" have not retired in any usual sense of the word. For example, one man, 61 at the time of the survey, "retired" from his former firm at age 57 to become the deputy director of a federal government bureau, an opportunity he said he made for himself by offering his services for a five-year period. His former employer records him as being retired, because he is drawing a company pension, but most people would consider that he is working at a second career.

Indeed, there is no very precise terminology to describe the status of persons leaving employment after 20, 30 or more years with one employer (as many of the retiree group have done), and who then begin to work for themselves or for another employer. Are they "retired," "partially retired," or not retired at all? One of the retirees says that he gains some income from buying, repairing and selling business machines, but adds that this is more of a hobby than a business. Is he retired?

The Conference Board survey begged the question of a definition of retirement by using a completely artificial definition. Cooperating firms selected the retirees to receive questionnaires. The mailing included an insert identifying the firm. The requested information "when you retired" and "at retirement" was defined in the questionnaire as the time when the respondent left the employ of that firm; "retirement" and "in retirement" were defined as the subsequent period, no matter how the respondent had used that time.

It is for this reason that the "retiree" group includes persons who say that "I am NOT retired." Indeed, 18 percent place themselves in that status (See Table 3) and, of those, 98 percent add: "And I like that." Thirty-six percent say they do some work, for pay or as a volunteer, "but not enough to interfere with my leisure." They are almost as satisfied with the arrangement. In spite of the fairly widespread belief that most managers would go on working forever if they could, almost half of this group of retired managers and professionals say "I do no work, for pay or as a volunteer," and 92 percent report that they like that.

Mandatory Retirement, Inflation and the Ages at which Employees Retire

In many situations, companies have specified an age at which employees must retire—usually 65. Typically, the benefits of corporate pension plans are coordinated with the benefits received from the federal social security system and full federal benefits become available at age 65. But

Table 3: Current Status and Retirees' Reactions to It[1]

Current Status	Number	Percent	Approve of Status
Retired; no work of any kind	1,635	46%	92%
Retired; some work	1,283	36	97
Not retired; paid work, volunteer work, or both	650	18	98

[1] Of the total of 3,679 retirees, 111 did not answer both parts of this item; only the replies of those respondents who answered both parts are included in the table.

Table 4: Age of Retirees at Retirement

Age	Number	Percent[1]	Age	Number	Percent
54 or younger	38	1%	63	272	7%
55	87	2	64	232	6
56	40	1	65	1,670	46
57	52	1	66	105	3
58	81	2	67	68	2
59	75	2	68	46	1
60	237	6	69	17	1
61	142	4	70	23	1
62	442	12	71 or older	23	1

Youngest at retirement: 45 years
Oldest at retirement: 80 years

[1] Percentages do not add to 100 because of rounding.
Note: 29 persons did not give their ages.

---

in most large U.S. companies, 65 is not the age at which most employees retire.

In most large companies, personnel officials have noticed a trend toward earlier and earlier retirement on the part of employees at all levels. Indeed, the average age of retirement in many large firms today is 60 years, or even younger. For some firms this has become a problem. One large utility, which employs over 33,000 persons, recently contacted The Conference Board seeking "horror stories" from this study that could be used to discourage early retirements. An executive of the utility explained: "We can count on the fingers of two hands the number of managers we have who are beyond 60 years of age."

The retirees in this study reflect the trend toward early retirement. As Table 4 shows, 47 percent retired before reaching 65 years of age; 46 percent retired at 65; and only 9 percent postponed retirement beyond 65.

Those figures, however, mask the trend toward earlier retirement and also the changes that may be occurring in that trend, as Table 5 indicates. Of those who retired before 1970, only 40 percent retired "early," while a majority (51 percent) retired at age 65, and 10 percent retired even later. Of those who retired in 1972, however, only 38 percent retired at age 65; 53 percent had retired before that age.

In 1973, when the national rate of inflation rose to 6.2 percent from the 3 to 4 percent that

Table 5: Changes in Age at Retirement in Recent Years

		Percent Retiring at Age:[2]			
Year of Retirement[1]	Number of Retirees	61 or younger	62 to 64	65	66 or older
1969 or before	1,351	20%	20%	51%	10%
1970	286	20	28	45	7
1971	354	22	27	44	7
1972	368	25	28	38	9
1973	406	18	29	46	7
1974	390	23	33	40	4
1975	348	22	33	41	5
1976[a]	137	17	27	49	7
	3,640				

[1] The year of retirement is an approximation. When they responded to the survey in 1976, retirees gave their ages and their ages at retirement. The difference subtracted from 1976 yields a "year of retirement" that should be correct to within an average of six months.
[2] The percentages do not add to 100 because of rounding.
[a] The first half of 1976 only; the survey was conducted in the summer.

had prevailed prior to that year, there was a shift in the trend. Only 47 percent retired "early" that year, while 46 percent retired when they reached 65. The picture becomes confused at this point, for in 1974 and 1975, when inflation was even more of a problem (rates of 11.0 percent and 9.1 percent respectively), the majority of retirees left "early" once more. The relatively few persons in the sample who retired in the year the survey was conducted (1976) show another change in direction: Almost half retired at the "normal" retirement age and only 44 percent left "early."

These year-to-year changes in the age at which this group of former managers retired, which seem to run counter to what one would expect from the changes in the inflation rate, become more explicable if one assumes that the decision to retire voluntarily before one is required to do so is not made lightly or on the spur of the moment. Inflation and the fear of continued inflation with its effect upon the adequacy of an estimated postretirement income, can be expected to cause an older employee to reconsider plans to retire earlier than he or she needs to. The shift of figures to the right in Table 5, from the "61 or younger" to the "62 - 64" column, and from that column to the "65" column, shows people postponing their retirement by a year of two or three in the expectation of building up larger pension credits while, perhaps, waiting to see what would happen to the nation's inflation rate.

That inflation is on the minds of these retirees is borne out by the number of comments made in response to the question: "If you could have one realistic improvement in the quality of your retirement, what would it be?"

* "End inflation."
* "Relate pensions to the cost of living."
* "Slow down the rise in the cost of living."
* "Freedom from the fear of huge medical expenses" (from retirees who say that their health is good).
* "Adequate income on which to live" (from a retiree whose income have been adequate when he retired fifteen years ago).

Comments of this general tenor rank second only to those of retirees who say they can think of no way to improve their retirement experience.

What happens to the inflation rate possibly will have a greater impact upon the age at which employees of large companies retire than will the recent enactment of sweeping federal legislation prohibiting mandatory retirement of employees in private enterprise before the age of 70. Among the American public there is support for the raising of the retirement age—and even stronger support for the elimination of mandatory retirement at *any* fixed age. In a survey of 5,000 households across the country, conducted for The Conference Board by National Family Opinion, Inc., in late 1977, 64 percent of the respondents oppose mandatory retirement at any age, 4 percent opt for age 70, while only 32 percent favor mandatory retirement at age 60 or 65.[2]

Opposition to mandatory retirement seems to be greatest among those furthest from retiring. In the survey of 5,000 households, three-quarters of the respondents aged 25 and under say that they oppose mandatory retirement at any age, while a bare majority of these 65 and over take that position. And in a survey of its readers conducted by *Retirement Living* magazine, 55 percent of the respondents who were already retired say that laws *requiring* retirement at a fixed age would be "desirable for most people," while 62 percent of those not yet retired believe that such laws "would not be desirable for most people."[3]

The Board's survey of retirees did not include a question about whether or not the person had retired voluntarily, but there was opportunity for comments. A very few respondents express anger or bitterness at having been forced to retire, not always because they had reached

---

[2]*Special Consumer Survey Report,* The Conference Board, November, 1977.

[3]"What's the Right Age for Retirement? How You Voted in Our Reader's Poll," *Retirement Living,* April, 1977.

retirement age. Many more, however, say that they wish that they had retired earlier than they had, and this comment is made even by some who retired before age 65.

As will be reported in more detail later, two-thirds of those retirees who are not now working have no desire to do so, and almost all of the remainder attach a number of conditions to their statement that they might be interested— particularly the condition that they would not have to work full time or all year. The image of the U.S. manager as a man who is lost without his job does not seem to square with the facts. The majority seem well pleased to have left "the eight-to-five rat race" behind them.

It would appear that the widespread opposition to retirement at age 65 is an opposition to *mandatory* retirement, not to retirement per se. People of all ages are demanding a greater voice in the decisions that affect them. Persons approaching retirement seem to be part of this phenomenon. They do not want an employer or a government telling them when they *must* retire. But, given adequate provision for retirement income, U.S. managers at least seem quite prepared to do so voluntarily.

Chapter 2
Income-Producing Work

A FORMER ENGINEER in a vegetable oil-processing firm acts as a consultant to several firms, here and abroad, dealing with processing problems and the purchase of equipment. He is 75 and has been "retired" for ten years. He enjoys helping the foreign companies, the travel and the income—but not when it interferes with his hunting and fishing.

A 65-year-old former chief executive of a manufacturing firm—retired one year—serves as a director of ten corporations and a stock exchange but still finds time to serve as an officer or a trustee of two major universities, a large city hospital, a national scholarship fund, and several other nonprofit organizations.

Another former chief executive, 77 and retired for 12 years, operates a tree-farming and cattle-raising ranch. He made his own opportunity for "after retirement" income-producing work by buying timber acreage and a cattle herd while still employed.

A former manufacturing manager, 72 and retired for eight years, works as a park arborist and florist for the small city he once served as unpaid mayor and councilman. He manages on a small income—to which social security benefits and his pension make a greater contribution than does his salary from the city. He says that he would like to get "more word, more often, of former associates in the only company I ever worked for."

A former sales manager, 65 and retired three years, works as a real estate broker, an occupation for which he studied after he retired. He also serves as a volunteer in a suicide prevention agency.

A former officer of a manufacturing company works a few months out of the year as a consultant on packaging problems. He would like more work than he now has. Seventy years of age, he has been retired for five years.

A former personnel manager, now 70 and retired since age 56, is the administrator of a nursing home. He currently runs the whole operation as well as serving on the board, but is giving increased responsibilities to his principal assistant because he wants more time for travel.

A former middle manager is a limited partner, with his son and one other man, in a retail store. He keeps the books and enjoys waiting on customers. He is 75 and has been retired for ten years.

A former manager, 65 and retired for three years, is the paid director of a sports league, scheduling baseball and basketball games and serving as an official. He says that he enjoys his current activities much more than his former work as a production manager in a manufacturing firm.

What Do They Do?

Clearly, there is a wide range of activities,

Table 6: Extent of Income-Producing Work during Retirement

	Number	Percent[1]
Presently Engaged in Work	1,070	29[a]
Self-employed		45[b]
Employed by outside organization		43
Both		12
Worked at Prior Time during Retirement	619	17
Self-employed		26[c]
Employed by outside organization		67
Both		6
Total who have worked for income at any time during retirement	1,689	46

[a] Based upon total of 3,679 retirees.
[b] Based upon the 1,070 retirees now engaged in income-producing work.
[c] Based upon the 619 retirees not now engaged who were at a prior time during retirement.
[1] Percentages may not add to 100 because of rounding.

from licensed fishing guide to university professor, in which former managers involve themselves when they choose to pursue paid employment in their "retirement" years. Many do choose to do so. As Table 6 shows, 1,689 of the 3,679 retirees responding to the survey (46 percent) are either now engaged in income-producing work or have been so engaged at some time since they retired.

Those who are currently employed are about equally divided between owner-managers of a business and employees of a business that is not owned by the retiree. That is not true of those retirees who had worked at some time since they retired but who were not employed at the time of the survey; 67 percent of this latter group had been employed by an organization they did not own.

Most of these retirees work in business; only about one in 20 works (for pay) in a nonprofit organization, in government, or in an academic institution. The government positions are, for the most part, positions on city councils, as mayors or town managers, or as heads of government agencies at a local level. Those in the field of education divide about equally between instructors or professors and those who work on the business side of the academic organizations—raising funds, managing the buildings and grounds department, running the business office. The majority of those working in education do so in junior and senior colleges and universities.

Those retirees who have continued in business divide about equally into owner-managers and employees. About a quarter of the "employees" serve on boards of directors, and in this group former chief executives predominate by a wide margin. The directors include five times as many former chief executives as would be expected from their numbers in the total survey group. In many cases they are continuing to serve on the boards on which they were members before they retired.

About 15 percent of the "employees" are officers of the companies that employ them. In this group former corporate officers (but not former chief executives) are overrepresented; former middle-level managers are underrepresented among current corporate officers. Some of these officers are also directors of other companies; they are included in the officer group because that is the activity that takes the greatest part of their time.

Most of the remaining "employees," about three out of five of the "employee" group of working retirees, hold mid-management positions similar to the ones they held prior to retiring. In a minority of the responses it appears that they are working for their former companies, but on a reduced schedule and with somewhat different responsibilities; many of these describe themselves as "consultants." An example is a former loan officer who works a few hours a week, throughout the year, on a bank's loan committee.

Some of the "employees," of course, have taken on work completely different from their former managerial careers. One is school bus driver; another drives a truck ("and I enjoy that," he adds); another supervises the sale of ski lift tickets; and still another works as a tee starter at a country club. Nonetheless, most of the "employees" continue to do managerial work in retirement.

Former bankers evidently find it easier to continue in paid employment after they retire, or else they have more desire to do so. Former bankers are overrepresented in all three groups of current "employees," and especially among the directors and corporate officers. Former bankers are only about one in eight of the total survey group, but they are about one in three of the directors and officers among the current "employees."

One's Own Retirement Business

Many managers in large businesses dream that when they retire they will run a small business of their own. About half of the retirees in this survey, who have engaged in income-producing work, have done just that. Of those, about two-thirds manage one-man operations.

About a quarter of those retirees who own their own businesses are engaged in the private practice of some profession or some business specialty. Former corporate legal counsels practice general law; former corporate accountants and comptrollers do some public accounting or assist individuals in the preparation of income tax returns; a former investment specialist in a bank now provides an estate-planning service to local businessmen. One former middle-level marketing research manager now conducts telephone marketing surveys from his home. These one-man businesses also include the man who buys, repairs and sells used business machines, a house painter, and a man who manages and owns an apartment complex.

Many of these businessmen are consultants. They differ from the "employees" who have that title in that they are not regularly employed by their former or any other single firm. Rather, they have offered their services to a number of occasional clients, which may include their former employers but is as apt to include former customers.

The larger businesses owned by retirees still tend to be small, at least in terms of employees, and almost half of them are farms—tree farms, crop farms and, especially, cattle ranches. The frequency of cattle farming as a retirement activity, particularly of former chief executives and corporate officers, may be related to the one-time popularity of cattle as a tax shelter for highly paid executives. Most of these ranchers say that they acquired their acreage and their stock while they were still employed. However, many of these retiree-ranchers say that they grew up on a ranch and have looked forward to getting back to the country after retiring.

Unlike the "employees," about two-thirds of the retirees managing their own businesses are working in fields unrelated to their former work. A former production manager runs a retail store, a former corporate sales officer now runs a beer and wine distributorship.

Again, former chief executives are over-represented among those retirees who are engaged in their own businesses. Among former professionals, engineers and physical scientists, as well as lawyers, stand out.

Age and the Prevalence of Paid Work

As might be expected, the age of the retirees has an influence upon whether or not they are currently engaged in income-producing work. Those 68 and younger are overrepresented among the retirees who continue in paid work, while those 71 and older are underrepresented (see Chart 1). However, even among those retirees aged 77 and above, 17 percent are continuing in income-producing work. In all the younger age groups, more than one in five retirees continue in some form of gainful employment.

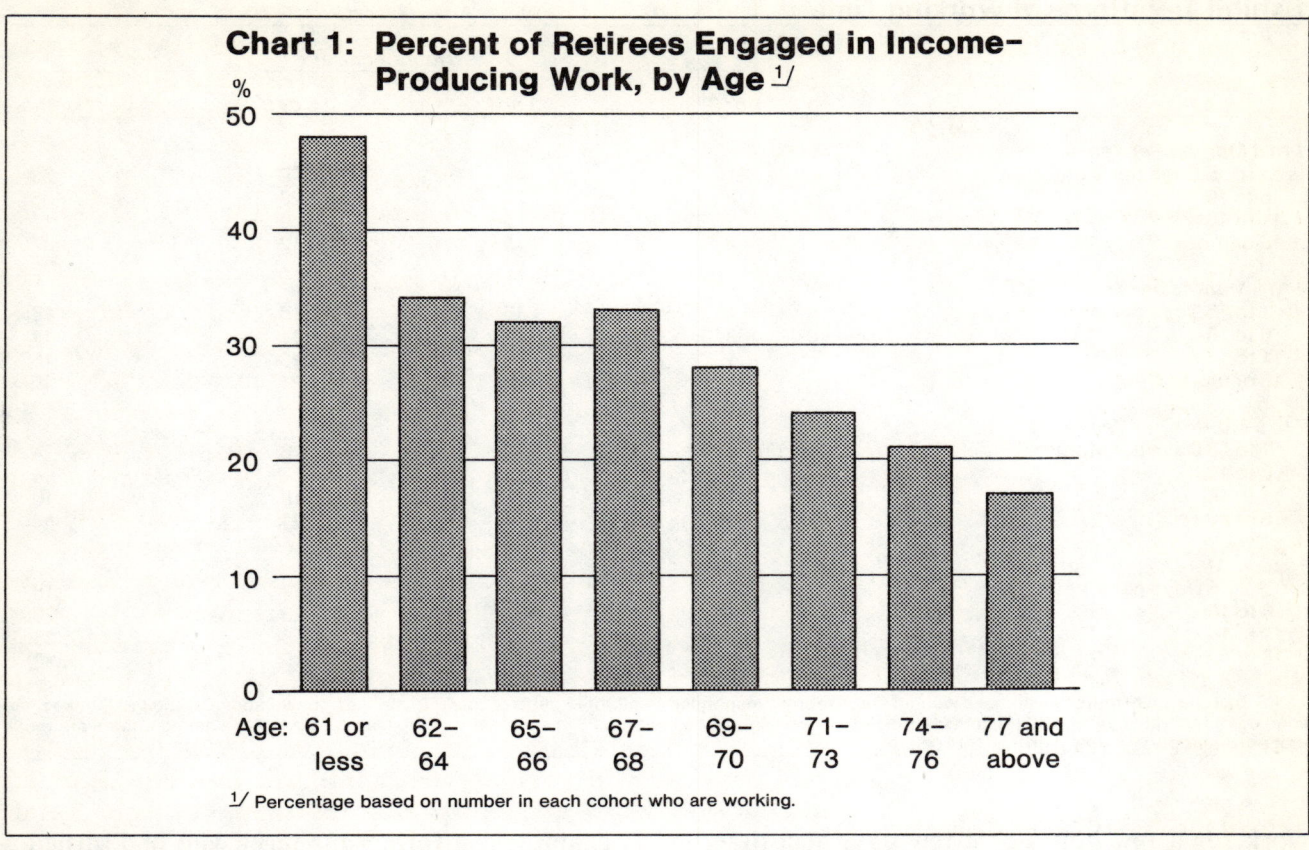

Chart 1: Percent of Retirees Engaged in Income-Producing Work, by Age [1]

[1] Percentage based on number in each cohort who are working.

These percentages are higher than the comparable figures for the population at large over the age of 65. In 1975, only 22 percent of the nation's white males over the age of 65 were in the labor force—that is, were working or were actively seeking work; of white males 70 and over, only 15 percent were in the labor force.[1]

Just over two-thirds of those retirees who have continued in gainful employment have held one job, if self-employment is defined as a "job." Since retiring, 18 percent have held two jobs and 13 percent have held three or more jobs. A number of the retirees with more than one job since retiring have worked at them simultaneously, most of them serving as consultants for several clients or serving on the boards of two or more companies. However, it is probable that most have held them in succession. The oldest retiree groups are the ones most apt to have held more than one job; if simultaneous multiple jobs were the rule, one would expect to find them about equally represented in all the age categories.

Time Spent in Income-Producing Work

Part-time work patterns predominate among the retirees who continue in income-producing employment. Only about a quarter of them work full-time—that is, seven or more hours per day, 16 or more days per month, for ten to 12 months of the year (see Exhibit 1). "Part-time" work, however, comes in a variety of patterns. In some cases, "occasional" work might be a more descriptive term, as, for instance, for the retirees included in the first line of the matrix in Exhibit 1. These persons may work for a full day when they are working, but they do so for only a few days a month and only for a few months of the year. Included in this group are retirees who take on infrequent consulting assignments for one or more clients. They may

[1] U.S. Department of Commerce, "Demographic Aspects of Aging and the Older Population in the United States," *Current Population Reports*; Series P-23, No. 59; Bureau of the Census, May, 1976.

Exhibit 1: Patterns of Working Time[1]

	Hours Per Day			
	1 or 2	3 or 4	5 or 6	7 or more
1 to 3 Months Per Year				
1 to 5 Days per Month:	51	46	48	38
6 to 10 " " "	2	20	26	25
11 to 15 " " "	1	5	9	17
16 or more " " "	2	6	12	67
4 to 6 Months per Year				
1 to 5 Days per Month:	4	16	10	18
6 to 10 " " "	2	21	14	14
11 to 15 " " "	1	11	23	15
16 or more " " "	—	8	21	45
7 to 9 Months per Year				
1 to 5 Days per Month:	3	10	3	4
6 to 10 " " "	—	8	7	4
11 to 15 " " "	1	11	18	10
16 or more " " "	2	4	31	34
10 to 12 Months per Year				
1 to 5 Days per Month:	33	39	27	18
6 to 10 " " "	12	31	29	20
11 to 15 " " "	1	43	38	26
16 or more " " "	9	51	99	392

[1] 1,616 of the 1,689 retirees who have worked since retiring responded to all three parts of this question, as shown above. If their responses had been equally divided among all the possibilities, there would have been about 25 in each entry of the matrix above. The shaded entries are those that are disproportionately high (i.e., 30 or more).

work for a few hours or a few days at a time, but most of their time is not spent in income-producing work. Slightly more than one in ten of the working retirees are included in the schedules shown in the first line of the matrix.

In contrast, a third of the retirees are included in the schedules shown in the last line of the matrix. Most of these are the 392 persons who are working full time. A significant number, however, work schedules that might be called "regular, part-time work." These retirees work throughout the year and most working days of the month, but for less than a full day. This is the pattern of a former corporate attorney, who now handles a small private practice involving fairly routine legal matters; he spends about a half day at this work for most working days of the year.

Another fairly common pattern of part-time work is that shown toward the bottom of the second column of the matrix. These persons work three or four hours a day, ten to 12 months of the year, but not for full months. An example is a former manager who had turned a hobby of woodworking and furniture repair into an income-producing business. He chooses to keep his volume low so that he does not have to spend all of his time at the work. He seldom works more than half a day in his shop, and he frequently closes down entirely for a week or two so that he and his wife can travel.

Indeed, it is only among the officers and other employees of companies not owned by the retirees that full-time work is the rule. About nine in ten officers work full time at their jobs and most of the rest devote at least half time. About half of the other "employees" work full-time schedules. But nine out of ten of the directors, three-quarters of the independent consultants, and half of those retirees in private professional practice spend less than half of a normal working schedule at their work. Even among those managing their own small businesses, about three out of five devote less than half of their time to this activity.

Working for income but at something less

than a normal full-time schedule has an obvious attraction for many retirees. Of the working retirees in this study, 60 percent report that they would like to continue with their present work at their present schedule or at even fewer hours but only 20 percent would like to work longer. Among those retirees who have not worked for income since retiring, but who say they might be interested in doing so, 69 percent attach the condition that they would not want to work full time or all year.

Most of the working retirees can choose the schedule that suits them. While many of the respondents admit that they welcome the income they derive from their work, few are completely dependent upon it. Income from investments or from company pensions are the major source of their funds. Thus, if they find their work loads too onerous, they have the option of reducing the load. While health may cause some to work less than they would like, few of these older persons have to work more than they find agreeable.

The age of the retiree has a bearing upon the schedule he works. Those who are still in their early 60's, or even younger, tend to work full-time if they choose to work during retirement; those who are 67 or older are overrepresented in the group working a half day or less, although they are proportionately represented in terms of days per month and months per year of income-producing work.

Similarity of Current and Former Work

For some of the retirees the reduction in working time is the major change from their preretirement careers; the nature of their work has not changed appreciably. Of the working retirees, 41 percent say that the jobs they now hold are substantially the same as the ones they held prior to retiring; another 26 percent report that their present work is similar to work they did at some earlier stage in their careers, although it differs from their final jobs. Only a third are involved now in work that is totally different from anything they ever did before retiring.

In some of these cases, the differences are rather great. A former corporate production officer has been involved full time since retiring in raising funds for a small liberal arts college. A former middle-level manager in the transportation industry says that his present work is as different from his former job "as government is different from industry." He is now an administrator in the Peace Corps. A man who owns and manages a small car rental agency was formerly a corporate officer in a manufacturing company. The former personnel manager of an insurance company now sells real estate. Another man explains that: "As an officer of an insurance company I had total responsibility for the overall marketing effort and directly supervised a number of field agencies. Now, as an assistant vice president of a bank, I advise people on money management."

Indeed, that distinction—between former line responsibilities for taking action and present roles as advisers of the actions that others should take—is the most significant difference between former jobs and current occupations for many of the retirees. Some welcome the change, but most who raise this distinction add that they preferred to be "on the firing line." They may like the reduced schedules that they work as consultants, but they do not gain the same satisfactions now that they merely give advice.

However, those who say that their present work is less enjoyable than the work they did prior to retiring are in the minority. Half of the working retirees say that they find their present work as enjoyable as they did their former jobs, while 28 percent are having greater satisfaction with work since they retired. "I do research work for fun now," says a scientist-consultant who formerly was engaged in research and development for a manufacturer of nondurable goods.

Satisfactions and Dissatisfactions

As a matter of fact, the total mentions of satisfactions with income-producing work made by the retirees (6,360) is over seven times the total mentions of specific dissatisfactions (894). Indeed, the most commonly checked item in a list of possible dissatisfactions—checked by 57 percent of the retirees—is a simple "None."

Factors intrinsic to the work itself are a major source of satisfaction for the retirees. (See Table 7.) More than half say that they gain satisfaction from the activities themselves; from the opportunity to continue to use the skills developed during their careers; and from the sense that they are doing something worthwhile. Only about a third report that they get satisfaction from the opportunity to develop new knowledge and skills. Whether that is because they do not value such opportunities or because their work does not offer many chances to learn new skills was not made clear; but the fact that many report their present work is substantially the same as work they have done in the past does suggest that the latter explanation is the correct one.

Factors concomitant to the actual job are also a source of satisfaction. Maintaining contact with other working people is a source of satisfaction for 58 percent of the working retirees, while merely having "something to do" is mentioned by 44 percent of them.

Finally, there is satisfaction from the work as a means to other ends. More than half of the retirees cite the income from their work as a source of satisfaction.

Less tangible, but obviously meaningful, factors were specifically mentioned by some of the retirees. One man said that his current work teaching production management is "the fulfillment of a lifelong ambition for an academic career." Another, who is also teaching, enjoys "helping young people to think bigger and bolder."

There are dissatisfactions, too, but they do not appear to loom as large. (See Table 8.) The fact that their work causes them to lose social security benefits to which they would otherwise be entitled is the only source of dissatisfaction reported by more than one in ten of the working retirees. "It is not fair to lose my social security benefits when I have paid for them in the past" says one retiree, voicing a common resentment over the perceived injustice as much as over the loss of income itself.

Table 7: Satisfactions Gained from Income-Producing Work

	Number	Percent
Intrinsic		
Use of knowledge and skills	1,048	62%
Enjoyment of work itself	1,042	62
Sense of accomplishment	997	59
Development of new knowledge and skills	603	36
Concomitant		
Contact with other workers	941	58
Something to do	732	43
Instrumental		
Income from work	997	59

Table 8: Dissatisfactions Associated with Income-Producing Work

	Number	Percent
No dissatisfactions	969	57%
Intrinsic		
Underutilization of best skills	139	8
Work too difficult for physical condition	16	1
Concomitant		
Not enough work	168	10
Insufficient time for personal interests	156	9
Insufficient pay for value of work	116	7
Too much work	41	2
Instrumental		
Loss of social security benefits	258	15

Finding Work

How did the retirees find the jobs they have held since retiring? In many cases the jobs found them; 36 percent say that they were contacted by former customers or business associates and were asked to take on the work that has occupied them (Table 9). This is the way a number of the consulting assignments came into being. Several men who have become sales representatives also have found opportunities coming to them, as is true of retirees now serving on the boards of companies with which they had dealings earlier in their business careers.

Personal and business friends and persons working for their former employer are the most common source of information about opportunities for work in retirement, with those three categories proving to be about equally frequent sources of leads. Advertisements in magazines or newspapers were the avenue to work for only 4 percent of the working retirees.

More than a quarter report that they created their own opportunities. One former corporate officer was doing a little consulting work, in the course of which he discovered a need for retrieval of computer data. Having set up a

Table 9: Retirees' Sources of Leads to Employment

	Number	Percent[1]
Information from others	953	56%
Former employer	333	20
Business friends	314	19
Personal friends	306	18
Job Offer made by former associates or customers	611	36
Opportunity self made	464	27
Information from "Help-wanted" advertising	64	4

[1] Percentages are based upon the 1,689 retirees who haved worked at any time during retirement. Percentages do not add to 100 because of multiple responses.

system that proved valuable for the decision making of his client, he realized that it could be valuable to others as well. He is now an officer of a data-retrieval business that he established.

A 62-year-old former middle-level personnel manager, who retired at 55, had long planned to work in land development when he retired early. He set about acquiring suitable parcels of land while he was still employed.

The professor of production management mentioned earlier, who is now 74, made a systematic search for a job when he retired 14 years ago. He considered various possibilities for his second career as a teacher and decided to investigate three universities. Resumes and personal letters drew favorable responses and invitations to visit from all three. He went only to the first, however. The situation there seemed to meet all his requirements, and he accepted the school's offer.

Sometimes a mere "cold" interview was all that was required to find suitable work. A former corporate sales officer in the insurance industry went into a bank and told an officer that he was looking for something to keep himself profitably occupied. He was hired to develop new business. A former banker also found a retirement career developing business for a bank, but in his case with an appropriate twist. After he and his wife moved to Florida, he discovered that many of his retired neighbors continued to maintain their bank accounts in the places from which they had migrated upon retirement. He sold a local bank the proposition that they should pay him a commission for any of these accounts that he managed to transfer to the local bank.

Not all attempts to find paid work have been successful, of course, All the retirees, whether or not they had worked since retiring, were asked if they had actively sought paid employment. Four hundred and seventy (13 percent) say that they have done so and, of those, 118 (or almost one in five) report that they were refused work on at least one occasion. On the other hand, 1,127 retirees (31 percent) say that they turned down opportunities for work.

Interest in Paid Work on the Part of Nonworking Retirees

As already reported, the majority of the retirees consider themselves completely or partially retired and say that they are happy with that condition. That could be "sour grapes" however. Therefore, the retirees who were not working for income at the time of the survey were asked if they would be interested in doing so. A very few flatly say "Yes"; two-thirds are defintely not interested; but almost a third might consider the idea (Table 10).

Those "maybe" responses are hedged with conditions. About a quarter would be interested only if they could earn enough to make the ef-

Table 10: Interest in Income-Producing Work Reported by Retirees Not Now Working

	Number	Percent[1]
Not interested	1,708	65%
Very interested, no conditions	66	3
Interested, but only under the following conditions:	814	31
Not full-time work, or for full year	559	69
Right sort of job	413	51
No loss of social security	230	28
Enough salary	229	28
Suited to physical condition	192	24

[1]The first three percentages are based on the 2,609 retirees who were not working for income at the time of the survey. The remaining percentages (below the short-ruled line) are based on the 814 retirees attaching conditions to their interest in paid work. These are multiple responses below the short-ruled line.

fort worthwhile, and the same number (but not necessarily all the same persons) would not take a job if it meant that they would lose their social security benefits. Almost a similar proportion express concern about the physical demands of a possible job. But a majority would be interested only in "the right sort of job," and for 69 percent of them that would mean work that did not demand full-time effort or a full-year's commitment.

Overwhelming, the "right job" is described as being consulting. Some retirees specify the field, such as "consultant in sales and/or marketing," "purchasing consultant," "consultant on railroad transportation," and "legal or financial consulting." The attraction of consulting as a retirement occupation, at least in the minds of these retirees, may be revealed by the man who says "management consulting at my convenience." Whatever the reason, consulting is mentioned as "the right sort of job" far more frequently than any other, although "registered pharmacist," "sales at retail in a small operation," "machinist" and such specific occupations are mentioned by some of the nonworking retirees who might be interested if the "proper" job were available. A few of these "possibly interested" retirees are very particular about the conditions under which they would be willing to go back to paid work; 48 of them (6 percent) check all five conditions as having to be met before they will interupt their leisure.

As mentioned earlier, a third of the working retirees have been involved with work that is different from any preretirement employment. That is not the same thing as being different from anything they have ever done, however. A considerable group of them developed the knowledge and skills that they use in their postretirement work while pursuing preretirement hobbies; and a number had done volunteer work that equipped them for their work in

Table 11: When and How Required Knowledge and Skills were Obtained[1]

	Number	Percent
Before Retiring		
Hobbies of other personal interests	165	30%
Formal study or training in a school	71	13
Volunteer work	47	8
Preretirement program of former employer	28	5
After Retiring		
Required knowledge and skill picked up on the job	247	45
Formal study or training in a school	45	8
Training program of postretirement employer	22	4
Volunteer work	19	3

[1]These responses were obtained only from the 553 working retirees who say that their postretirement work differs from any preretirement work they ever did. Percentages are based upon that number. The numbers will not total to 553, nor will the percentages total to 100 percent, because of multiple responses.

retirement (Table 11). One in five undertook formal study to gain needed training, either before or after the retirement date. Relatively few were assisted in preparing for retirement careers through the preretirement programs sponsored by their previous employers. Preretirement counseling programs are being presented by a growing number of U.S. companies today but they were relatively rare at the time this group of former managers retired. Almost half, however, had no problem learning how to do the work in which they have been involved; they say that they merely picked up the skills they needed on the job.

INCOME-PRODUCING WORK 17

Chapter 3
Serving Others Through Voluntary Work

THE MIDDLE CLASS is the traditional source for the armies of people who staff the nation's voluntary charitable, cultural, social and political organizations. The predominantly middle-class retirees who participated in the Board's study run true to this form; 1,567, or 43 percent, have worked as volunteers at some time since they retired (Chart 2). This is a slightly smaller percentage of the total group than the 46 percent who have engaged in remunerative employment.

A higher percentage continue as *active* volunteer workers, however; 1,241 (79 percent of the volunteers) say that they are currently working in one or more voluntary programs, while only 1,070 (63 percent) of those who have engaged in paid work while in retirement still do so.

What Do They Do?

Most of the retirees who engage in volunteer work do so through organizations of some type. Only a very few mention individual services that they perform. One man says that he assists the owner of the building in which he lives with maintenance and repairs; another does carpentry and plumbing for other retirees at no charge; still another repairs appliances for his neighbors and says that he "enjoys seeing things become whole." A former middle manager in a bank is helping a widow in his neighborhood with her financial matters. It is probable that more of the retirees perform such "neighborly" services than show up in the survey figures because several who did list such services raised the question of whether or not the Board meant such activities to be included as "volunteer work."

Nonetheless, the vast majority of the retiree volunteers work through organizations and, of those, about three-quarters do so through organizations primarily intended to help others. About a quarter of all retirees who "volunteer" serve church organizations, primarily their local congregations, and another quarter work for local social service agencies, such as the Boy Scouts, drug rehabilitation agencies, "Meals on Wheels" programs, or the Red Cross.[1] Ten percent or fewer of the retirees work for local hospitals or health clinics; for business-related agencies, such as SCORE (the Service Corps of Retired Executives of the Federal Department of Commerce) and the International Executives Service Corps, as well as industrial development groups; or for government-related organizations such as airport commissions, conservation districts, and police and fire commissions.

---

[1]"Meals on Wheels" is the name commonly applied to programs funded under Title VII of the Older Americans Act of 1965. This Title, administered by the Administration on Aging of the Department of Health, Education, and Welfare, makes funds available for preparing and delivering meals that are nutritionally balanced (a requirement of the Act) to housebound persons 60 years of age or older who would not otherwise have a daily hot meal. The programs are usually run by a local nonprofit social service agency, "golden age club," or other organization under contract to a local government unit, which gets it funds from the Federal Government through the state.

Chart 2: Extent of Volunteer Work

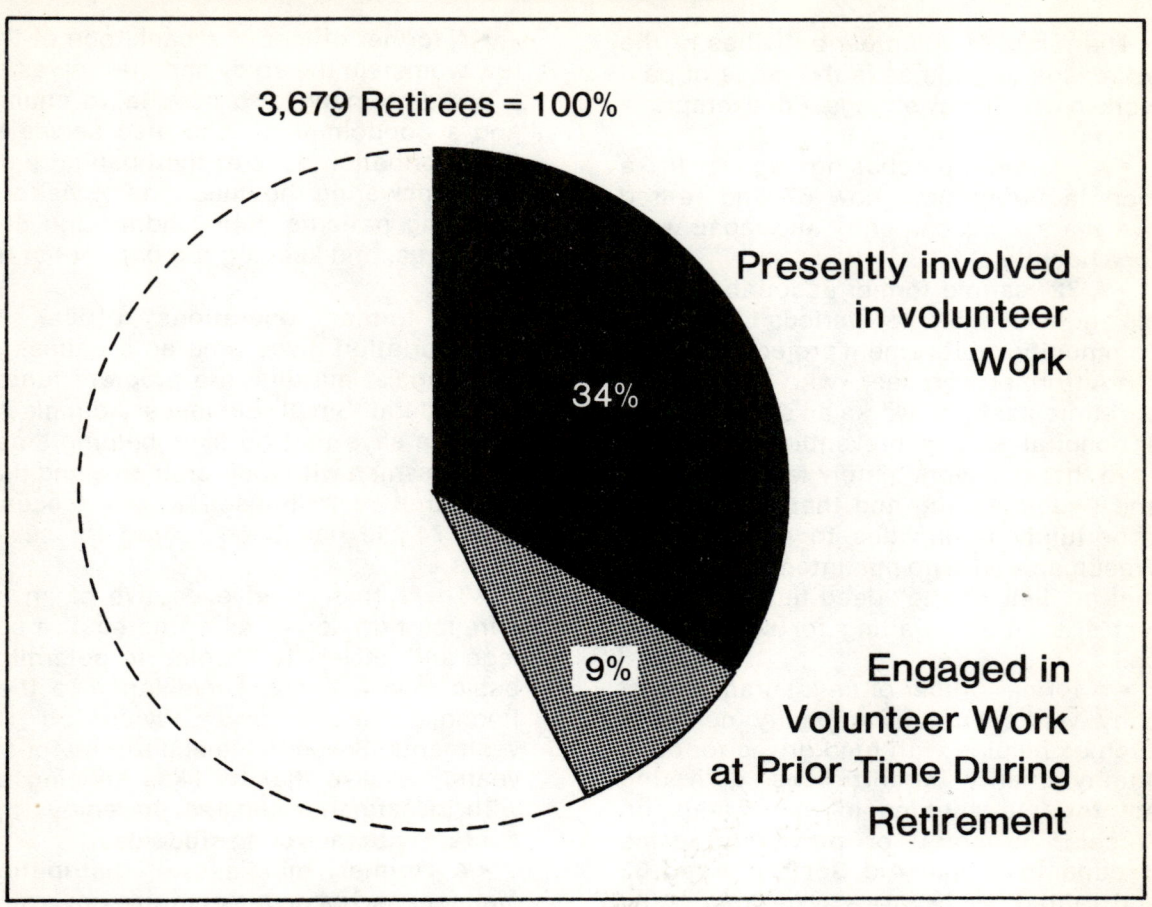

Fewer than one in 20 retirees work for educational institutions, and then primarily as trustees or fund-raisers.

Almost a quarter of the volunteering retirees do free work for groups that, in some sense at least, are partially self-serving. Included in this category are such organizations as country clubs, sports and social clubs, and groups devoted to certain hobby activities. Retiree clubs are another example of partially "self-interest" organizations that engage the volunteer activities of these retirees, although many retirees provide service to others through such groups—helping with tax return preparation, for example. Condominium and cooperative apartment associations and homeowners' associations are also included here among the "self-interest" category of volunteer organizations.

Volunteering Began Before Retirement

The majority of the retirees who have been engaged in volunteer work are merely continuing a practice begun before retirement. Sixty-nine percent of them had been volunteers during their business careers. Almost three-quarters have continued to do substantially the same sort of volunteer work in retirement (Table 12), although they may have begun to work for different organizations after they retired.

The "substantially similar" work tends to be the sort that managers frequently engage in: serving on boards of directors or trustee boards of hospitals, social agencies, and cultural in-

SERVING OTHERS THROUGH VOLUNTARY WORK

> **Varieties of Volunteer Jobs Performed**
>
> The range of volunteer activities of the retirees is as wide as is the range of paid work in which they engage. For example:
>
> • A former purchasing agent in a manufacturing firm, now 67 and retired five years, does carpentry and repair work for a hospital.
>
> • A 72-year-old former accountant uses his "general skills" on various Lions Club community improvement projects.
>
> • A former engineer, who also has a part-time paid job, works as a volunteer in a hospital suicide-prevention clinic. He says that this work merely takes patience and understanding and that he likes the opportunity it provides to meet people. Presumably with no pun intended, he says that he dislikes the "dead time" when he just sits around waiting for someone to call.
>
> • A former officer of an insurance company works "in any capacity needed," such as helping with fund drives for community charity organizations, delivering hot food to shut-ins in the "Meals on Wheels" program, or providing advice through the Legal Aid Society. Aged 62 and retired for two years, he also golfs, boats and hikes, does a good bit of reading, and spends a month or more annually traveling.
>
> While the range of activities is wide, most of the voluntary activities of the retired managers are such that they draw upon their managerial knowledge and the skills they developed during their careers. For instance:
>
> • A former vice president of production is the chairman of a long-range planning committee for a new retirement community in Florida.
>
> • A former officer of a bank, one of the few women in the study sample, serves as a board member for a hospital, a church and a condominium. She also serves at the information desk at the hospital part-time, answering the questions of visitors, assisting patients during admission and discharge, and keeping the patient list up to date.
>
> • A former operations officer in transportation gives time as a counselor on financial matters in a program run by the federal Small Business Administration. He says that he likes helping small businessmen with their problems and that he learns more himself in the process. Now 74, he has been retired for seven years.
>
> • The former chief executive of an insurance firm serves as a trustee of a college and university, helping to determine basic policy, giving surveillance to their financial affairs and advice on investments. Seventy-one and retired for six years, he says that he likes keeping up with investments and that he enjoys the contact with the young students.
>
> • A former middle-level distribution manager serves on his church's governing council, overseeing general church business and helping with the planning of its educational program. The work calls for his business and human relations skills, he says, and he likes the participation in meaningful work but he dislikes the regular schedule it forces upon him.
>
> • A 78-year-old former chief executive serves off and on as a consultant with the International Executive Service Corps, assisting with the management problems of companies in developing countries. He likes his expense-paid travel and "seeing companies prosper as a result of my help."

stitutions; advising groups on their business affairs and financial matters; working with local businessmen's groups. More than half of the retiree volunteers work on boards and committees in the organizations they serve, although this rises to three-quarters among those in the

Table 12: Volunteer Work Before and After Retirement Compared

	Number	Percent[1]
Volunteer work before retiring	1,075	69%
No volunteer work before retiring	492	31
Pre- and Postretirement Volunteer Work Compared:		
Nature of work		
Substantially similar		73
Substantially different		27
Location of Volunteer Work		
Same organizations as before retirement		41
Same organizations as before retirement, plus one or more new organizations		28
Different organizations		32

[1]The responses at the top of the table come from the 1,567 retirees who have worked as volunteers at any time since retiring; those percentages are based on that number. The percentages in the lower part of the table, dealing with comparisons of pre- and postretirement volunteer activity, are based upon the 1,075 retirees who had engaged in volunteer work before retiring. Percentages do not add to 100 because of rounding.

government-related organizations and in the condominium-homeowners' category. In the retiree organizations, on the other hand, only about a quarter of the volunteer retirees primarily serve on the boards and more than half provide direct service to other retirees.

Almost a quarter of the retiree volunteers perform other work for their organizations similar to work performed during their business careers. Many former accountants, for instance, actually keep the books and handle the financial affairs of churches, social agencies, and other organizations. Some, with previous experience in maintenance, manage the building maintenance and repair programs of their organizations. A number give ongoing investment advice or handle the portfolios of larger social agencies.

About a quarter of the retiree volunteers provide services that are unrelated to their previous careers. Some teach for the Red Cross, or teach safe boating for the United States Power Squadrons or for the Coast Guard Auxiliary. A number do carpentry or other maintenance work for churches, hospitals, cerebral palsy centers, and children's homes. Many use their cars to drive patients to hospital or clinic appointments or to deliver "Meals on Wheels" to elderly persons who cannot leave their homes to provide for themselves. Some serve as "Big Brothers" to youngsters or as counselors in drug rehabilitation programs. A number mentioned serving as unpaid consultants to small businessmen in the SCORE program. These are the jobs that tend to fall into the "different-from-previous-volunteer-work" category; most could not have been fitted into a normal business day prior to retirement.

Similarly, few employed managers or professionals can take the time to travel to a developing country for a month or more to provide consulting services to a local businessman, as a number of the retirees have done under the aegis of the International Executive Service Corps, gaining personal satisfaction while using their accumulated business expertise to help someone else.

For many older persons retirement has been a liberation, not from work, but from the typical working schedules that prevented them from engaging in activities they now find meaningful. "I'm not retired, I'm reoriented," says one busy retiree who now spends his time with the Institute of Retired Professionals at the New School for Social Research in New York City.[2] Institute members are both faculty and students for the special courses they present for themselves in their respective professional fields.

Which Retirees Volunteer?

As in the case of the retirees who engage in income-producing work, those who volunteer their services differ in some respects from those who do not. Former managerial employees, as opposed to former professionals, are overrepresented among the volunteers. And, among the former managers, corporate officers (but not chief executives) are overrepresented; former middle managers do not volunteer at the same rate as do the officers.

[2]Reported in the *New York Times,* Jaunary 5, 1977.

In terms of the industry in which the retirees worked prior to retiring, all are about proportionately represented, with the exception of former bankers. They are overrepresented in all categories of volunteer organizations and especially in the "self-interest" category—the social, sports and country clubs; the condominium and homeowners' groups; and the retiree organizations.

The educational level of the volunteers is slightly higher than that of the nonvolunteers. A somewhat higher proportion are college graduates or have advanced degrees.

The median income of the retirees is slightly higher than that of the retirees who have not volunteered their services, but the distribution is bimodal. The volunteers are overrepresented at both the low and the high ends of the income range. Slightly lower than average incomes predominate among the retirees active in church organization, and homeowners' groups. Higher than average incomes are typical of those who do their volunteer work for hospitals. But as a percentage of their preretirement incomes, the current incomes of the various groups of retiree-volunteers are about the same—61 to 70 percent—the exceptions being those who engage in service with their churches.

Although their incomes tend to be lower than that of other retiree-volunteers, the average income is 71 to 80 percent of preretirement earnings.

As might be expected, those retirees who are active with volunteer work report better health than do those who are not. Among the volunteers, twice as many may say that their health and general physical condition are better now than in the decade before they retired than say that they are worse; for the nonvolunteers the reverse is true, although not to as great an extent. However, both groups seem to be in reasonably good health; about three-quarters of the volunteers and two-thirds of the non-volunteering retirees say that their health is "about the same." (See Chart 5, page 43, for details on health.)

The age of a retiree has an impact on his or her readiness to volunteer services to others. Retirees begin to be underrepresented as volunteers when they reach age 74. Those 65 to 73 years of age are the most active group of volunteers; in this group are those who spend the greatest amount of their time at volunteer activities, and who are most apt to say that they would like to continue their current level of volunteer activity—or to do even more. Retirees under the age of 65 are not as involved in volunteer work; that group is overrepresented among those who are engaged full time in income-producing work, and they may simply not have the time to volunteer.

Time Spent at Volunteer Work

Only 1 percent of the retirees who volunteer their services work full time at these activities, in contrast with the situation of those who engage in income-producing work; of these individuals, almost a quarter work full time. Full-year and part-time work is the prevailing pattern for the volunteers (Exhibit 2 on p. 23).

Sixty-three percent of the volunteering retirees have responsibilities that continue ten to twelve months of the year. Of those, three-quarters work for ten days a month or less, and *of those* 85 percent work a half day or less when they are engaged in volunteer work. Thus, volunteer work is a continuous but part-time activity for 41 percent of the volunteers. Of the remainder, 518 work lesser schedules while only 295 work more than ten days a month or more than four hours a day throughout the year.

While continuous but part-time work is the prevailing pattern, that does not mean that the rest of the retiree's time is spent in a rocking chair or its modern equivalent. Four hundred and sixteen (34 percent) of those retirees who are volunteers at present are also currently engaged in income-producing work. (Those same 416 retirees represent 39 percent of the retirees engaged in paid work.) This helps to account for the part-time nature of the volunteer schedules many of them follow. Most of the others are busy with a multitude of avocational activities. It is the retirees working for income or as volunteers, however, who report the greatest satisfaction with retirement.

Exhibit 2: Patterns of Time Spent in Volunteer Work[1]

	Hours Per Day			
	1 or 2	3 or 4	5 or 6	7 or more
1 to 3 Months Per Year				
1 to 5 Days per Month:	108	59	24	7
6 to 10 " " "	8	18	7	4
11 to 15 " " "	2	4	1	2
16 or more " " "	—	3	12	23
4 to 6 Months per Year				
1 to 5 Days per Month:	20	17	3	1
6 to 10 " " "	6	18	5	1
11 to 15 " " "	—	4	3	—
16 or more " " "	1	5	4	8
7 to 9 Months per Year				
1 to 5 Days per Month:	21	43	4	2
6 to 10 " " "	6	21	13	—
11 to 15 " " "	—	11	8	—
16 or more " " "	1	4	5	1
10 to 12 Months per Year				
1 to 5 Days per Month:	203	169	40	15
6 to 10 " " "	80	123	39	4
11 to 15 " " "	15	64	16	1
16 or more " " "	21	38	27	15

[1] Of the 1,567 retirees who have worked as volunteers at some time since they retired, 1,388 answered all parts of this question. If their responses had been equally divided among all the possibilities in the matrix above, there would have been about 21 in each entry above. The shaded entries are those that are disproportinatley high (i.e., 30 or more).

Satisfactions and Dissatisfactions

The satisfactions gained by retirees from their volunteer work are similar to those they report getting from their income-producing efforts: Enjoyment of the activities themselves, the chance to continue using the knowledge and skills developed during their careers, and the opportunity to maintain contact with other volunteers and working people—are all satisfactions mentioned by a significant number of the retirees (see Table 13 on p. 24). By far the most widely expressed satisfaction comes with the sense of accomplishment from their volunteer activities; 85 percent of the retirees cite this. This is in striking contrast to the 59 percent of retirees who say that they get a sense of accomplishment when they are engaged in income-producing work. It may be that one of the respondents speaks for many of these volunteers when he says: "It's rewarding doing something for nothing."

Indeed, the sense of accomplishment is the only satisfaction listed in Table 14 that is cited by retirees more frequently in connection with volunteer activities than with paid work. Otherwise, a greater percentage of retirees who are working for income than of retirees who are volunteers enjoy the activities themselves, for instance, or relish the chance to develop new knowledge and skills that their work provides.

As with paid work, "none" is the response given by the majority to describe the dissatisfactions they find associated with their volunteer activities (see Table 14 on p. 24). Only about one in ten mentions that the work cuts into the time one could spend with one's family or that the volunteer work does not make use of one's greatest skills. A mere 2 percent of the retirees who volunteer complain that one should be paid for the useful work one does. Obviously, most who feel that way simply do not volunteer.

Indeed, people who do not really want to volunteer their services usually do not do so. It is true that some people get involved in volunteer work through social pressure, because

SERVING OTHERS THROUGH VOLUNTARY WORK

Table 13: Satisfactions Gained from Volunteer Work

	Number	Percent
Intrinsic		
Sense of accomplishment	1,307	83%
Enjoyment of volunteer activities themselves	813	52
Development of new knowledge and skills	726	46
Use of current knowledge and skills	360	23
Concomitant		
Contact with other volunteers and working people	739	47
Something to do	450	29

[1]These responses were drawn from the 1,567 retirees who have engaged in volunteer work at any time during retirement; percentages are based on that number. Percentages do not add to 100 because of multiple responses.

they find it hard to say no when asked to help with a good cause. Others, who want some volunteer work, find that they have too much of a good thing after they have taken positions on several boards, committees and projects. But when the dissatisfactions become too great, volunteers have an out—they quit.

Thus, a 72-year-old former vice president of production will *not* again serve as a consultant overseas. "I've had a bellyfull," he says. His objection is not to the assignment—advising on the construction of a cotton mill—but to the living conditions in the developing country in which he worked.

Similarly, a former investment specialist has been "soured on all volunteer work" by his experience as an officer of a civic organization in a large housing subdivision. He represented the organization on matters of zoning, street changes, and community improvement projects, with "lots of free advice" from his neighbors. He sums up the experience: "It took more patience than I have. It was too much of a hassle. I got out as soon as I could."

Other retirees find some aspects of their work unappealing even though, on balance, they enjoy it. For example, a former accountant, now 67, serves as janitor and does light maintenance for his church at the invitation of the minister. While he dislikes "the congregation, which literally demolishes the church on weekends," he finds the job rewarding because of the "results—the church is clean and it was once untidy." Similarly, a retired officer of a manufacturing company serves as a city councilman at so small a fee that he considers it volunteer work. He gets satisfaction from "service to the city and from working with concerned citizens and city employees," even though he dislikes the constant "petty complaints and self-oriented appeals to the council."

Volunteer work, then, has its pluses and minuses—but overall the volunteers in this study find it a rewarding and worthwhile thing to do. In fact, 61 percent of the retirees want to continue with their present volunteer work. Some of the respondents—14 percent—would like to do even more of the same kind of work. A few think they are overcommitted; 8 percent of the retirees would like to continue with their present volunteer work, but to do somewhat less of it. Among these latter volunteers are the oldest retirees in the sample.

Eight percent of the retirees would like to do some other type of volunteer work than that they are now engaged in but, comparing their responses, they would merely trade jobs. Where one person who serves on a number of boards

Table 14: Dissatisfactions Associated with Volunteer Work[1]

	Number	Percent
No dissatisfactions	1,143	73%
Intrinsic		
Underutilization of highest skills	117	7
Concomitant		
Insufficient time for personal interests	81	5
Not enough work	74	5
One should be paid for useful work	26	2

[1]These responses were drawn from the 1,567 retirees who have engaged in volunteer work at any time during retirement; percentages are based on that number. Percentages do not add to 100 because many retirees gave no responses while others gave more than one.

would like to provide direct service to clients—"to have more contact with the people"—another who is currently counseling dropouts would like to work on his agency's governing board—"to make use of my management skills."

How Were They Recruited?

As mentioned earlier, more than two-thirds of the retiree volunteers had been engaged in volunteer work before retiring. Of these, 47 percent have been involved in their recent volunteer activities because they had been involved in similar work in the past (Table 15). About half of the volunteers, however, were directly recruited for their recent work—that is, were approached by representatives of the volunteer organizations and asked to serve. This direct personal appeal for help is by far the most effective method for recruiting these former managers. Much less frequently mentioned is contact by personal or business friends who talk about the work of the organizations. Articles, newspaper and radio programs, and advertisements appealing for help attracted only 8 percent of the volunteers.

Table 15: How Retirees were Recruited for Volunteer Work

	Number	Percent
Contact by volunteer organization representatives	760	49%
Had been doing similar work before retiring	733	47
Through Friends		
Personal	388	25
Business	136	9
Media		
Magazine or newspaper article about work of volunteer organization	74	5
Advertisement appealing for volunteers	29	2
Television or radio program about work of volunteer organization	14	1

[1] These responses were drawn from the 1,567 retirees who have been engaged in volunteer work at any time during retirement; percentages are based on that number. Percentages do not add to 100 because of multiple responses.

If voluntary agencies could find a way to reach retired managers with a personal appeal they might well increase their supply of active volunteers. Of those retirees who are not now engaged in volunteer work, more than a third might be interested in such activities, although almost all of them attach conditions to their interest (Table 16). The most frequently mentioned condition is that the work would not take full time or involve the person all year. Inasmuch as almost all the volunteer work now being done by retirees meets that condition, this does not seem to pose a major problem to the working out of mutually satisfactory arrangements between retirees and voluntary agencies.

Table 16: Interest in Volunteer Work Reported by Retirees Not Now Involved[1]

	Number	Percent
Not interested	1,383	60%
Very interested, no conditions	80	3
Interested, but only under the following conditions:	834	36
Not full-time work, or for full year	418	50
Right sort of job	369	44
Respect for organization	321	38
Suits physical condition	195	23
Can afford time	165	20

[1] Of the 2,376 retirees who reported that they were not engaged in volunteer work at present, 2,297 responded to this question; the first three percentages in the table are based on the latter figure. The remaining percentages, below the short-ruled line, are based upon the 834 persons who attached conditions to their interest in volunteer work.

"The right sort of work" is also a conditional factor for many of the retirees. Again, this is defined in so many ways that most desires could be accommodated usefully by some agency. "Easy work of value to others," says one man. Others make such specifications as these: "any job that I could feel is making a contribution to society"; "work with local agencies in welfare or with the Red Cross"; or "work in a hospital or with children." More specific definitions of "the right sort of job" include: "assignments in my field under some international volunteer executive group"; "something concerned, in an

SERVING OTHERS THROUGH VOLUNTARY WORK

enlightened way, with increasing general awareness of the desirability of our kind of economic society"; and "work with the Chamber of Commerce or Board of Trade."

"Any worthwhile charitable organization" was written in as a condition by one retiree who probably speaks for the 38 percent checking this item: "If I knew of an organization whose purpose I respected." Inasmuch as volunteer organizations have not been able to attract many volunteers through articles, radio or television programs describing their work, the reaching of retirees who might be interested in serving poses a problem for the volunteer groups. Personal contact by organization representatives has been the most effective means, but how can the organizations establish that personal contact?

Many, perhaps most, business firms will not reveal the names and addresses of their retired employees to outsiders. (Two-thirds of the firms that cooperated with The Conference Board in this study chose to mail the questionnaires themselves so that the names and addresses of the retirees would not be divulged to the Board.) Agencies requiring the services of volunteers, no matter how laudable their goals, usually cannot get lists of either retirees or active employees from companies.

Some firms attempt to go half way in serving the interests of both their retired employees, who might want opportunities for meaningful volunteer work, and of the agencies needing such help. As with the example of the Board's questionnaire, these firms send information to retirees about voluntary agencies and about the work that needs to be done, leaving it to the retirees to make contact if they are interested in doing so. Some companies that sponsor retirement clubs for former employees suggest to voluntary agencies that they contact club officers with their information and appeals; the agencies might be asked to send speakers to the club to talk with members. One major insurance firm pays a small stipend to some of its former employees to investigate volunteer opportunities and to call to the attention of other retirees those that seem worthwhile. It also provides a small stipend to the retirees who choose to engage in such volunteer work of service to the community.

Clearly, opportunities for volunteer activity exist for most retirees who seek it. Of 496 who report that they have actively sought out opportunities for volunteer work, only 23 (5 percent) say that they have been refused. In contrast, 779 retirees have themselves turned down opportunities to engage in volunteer activities.

Lack of skills for performing their volunteer assignments does not seem to present a problem for retired managers and professionals. Almost all had acquired at least some of the knowledge and skill they have used in their volunteer work before they retired from their paid employment, from previous volunteer work or merely from the pursuit of their personal interests (Table 17). For the most part, whatever else was needed in the way of specialized knowledge was just picked up on the job. Only 7 percent of the retirees who have volunteered learned what they needed from a training program sponsored by the volunteer agency.

Inasmuch as the types of work that the retirees have done is similar in many respects to

Table 17: When and How Required Knowledge and Skills were Obtained[1]

	Number	Percent
Before Retiring		
Previous paid employment	603	38%
Volunteer work	529	34
Hobbies or personal interests	428	27
Preretirement program of previous employer	6	a
After Retiring		
Required knowledge and skills just picked up on the volunteer job	668	43
Training program of the volunteer organization	115	7

[1] These responses were drawn from the 1,567 retirees who have engaged in volunteer work at any time during retirement; percentages are based on that number. Percentages do not add to 100 because of multiple responses.

[a] Less than one-half of one percent.

their preretirement jobs, it is to be expected that their previous work experience would be the predominant source of their skills. It is this store of managerial and professional experience that makes this retiree group a valuable national resource.

Chapter 4
Avocations

ABOUT HALF OF the former managers in this study classify themselves as "completely retired"; they do no work, either for income or as volunteers. Another third report that they do a bit of work "but not enough to interfere with my leisure." And, as previously shown, even those who are engaged in paid or volunteer work generally have considerable time left over for nonwork activities. How do these formerly active people fill the hours that are no longer programmed by the demands of a job?

They do not sit around twiddling their thumbs. They travel, garden, play golf, and go hiking. They pursue the arts of calligraphy and lapidary. As this report was being written a questionnaire was received with the note: "Sorry this is a year late. I've just been too busy to get to it before this." Another questionnaire arrived a few months earlier, also with an apology and the explanation: "We are nine months into an eighteen-month tour of the world and this just caught up with us." These retirees find ways to occupy their time.

Sports

Golf is a popular pastime with the retirees; for a few it is a consuming passion. More than three out of four of the retirees regularly engage in some active sport, with golf being clearly the most popular (Table 18). Walking or hiking is another sport enjoyed by about a third of those who engage in sports. Fishing, swimming, hiking and walking appeal to many retirees; boating or sailing, bowling, hunting and tennis

Table 18: Participation in Active Sports[1]

	Number	Percent
Regular engagement in active sports	2,826	77%
Sports		
Golf	1,798	64
Fishing	1,220	43
Swimming	992	35
Hiking and walking	957	34
Boating and sailing	498	18
Bowling	426	15
Hunting	364	13
Tennis	185	7
Time spent		
Under 5 hours per week	721	26
5 to 15 hours per week	1,500	53
16 to 30 hours per week	505	18
Over 30 hours per week	54	2
When interest developed		
Many years ago	2,502	89
In the years just before retirement	142	5
Since retirement	153	5

[1] The percentages given for those who engage in active sports (above the short-ruled line) are based on the total retirees. The other percentages (below the short-ruled line) are based on the number who engage in sports. The percentages below the line do not always add to 100 because a few respondents in each group did not answer all the subsidiary questions.

are enjoyed by fewer of them. Ice-skating, bicycling and calisthenics were mentioned by a number of people; few mentioned such relatively uncommon sports as fox hunting and the Scottish ice-rink sport of curling.

About nine out of ten of the retirees who engage in sports have been interested in sports

Table 19: Participation in Avocational Activities, by Age of Retirees

Age Group	Number of Retirees	Sports	Hobbies	Study	Travel
61 and under	217	85%	81%	20%	82%
62—64	405	83	82	20	85
65—66	550	80	84	15	86
67—68	644	80	84	16	85
69—70	524	78	82	17	86
71—73	578	77	79	20	89
74—76	384	72	80	18	82
77 and older	352	57	72	17	76
All ages	3,654	77	82	17	85

Percent of Each Age Group Participating in: Sports, Hobbies, Study, Travel

for many years. Only 10 percent of the retirees took up sports just before retiring or subsequently.

One might expect that participation in active sports would decrease with age; indeed that is the case with these former managers and professionals. The degree of participation, however, is high at all ages (Table 19). Among the youngest retirees—those of age 61 and younger—85 percent engage regularly in some sport. That percentage drops in each subsequent age group until only 57 percent of the oldest group—those 77 and older—regularly engage in sports activities. While that is a marked decrease from 85 percent, it still means that almost three in five of these oldest retirees have not only the time but also the energy and interest to participate regularly in sports.

Hobbies

In addition to sports, most of the retirees also pursue one of more hobbies. Four out of five retirees spend some of their time in this way (Table 20). Gardening and reading are the most common of these leisure activities but playing cards, woodworking, cabinetmaking, furniture-finishing, and photography also have considerable numbers of devotees. Over half of each group spends from five to 15 hours a week engaged in hobbies.

In a relatively few cases the hobbies are also a source of income—but it is usually a minor source, as in the case of the man who buys, repairs and sells business machines and a professional skeet-shooting instructor. The income is used primarily to support the hobby; the activities are valued for themselves.

Again as with sports, the hobbies of the retirees generally represent long-standing interests. In most cases they were not taken up after retirement merely to fill empty time.

Table 20: Pursuit of Hobbies[1]

	Number	Percent
Regular pursuit of one or more hobbies	2,981	82%
Hobbies		
Gardening	1,859	63
Reading	1,624	54
Cards—bridge, poker, etc.	1,229	41
Woodworking, furniture-finishing	761	26
Photography	723	24
Collecting—coins, stamps, etc.	408	14
Painting, sculpture	150	5
Lapidary, jewelry making	73	2
Time spent		
Under 5 hours per week	496	17
5 to 15 hours per week	1,615	54
16 to 30 hours per week	672	23
Over 30 hours per week	159	5
When interest developed		
Many years ago	2,688	90
In the years just before retirement	123	4
Since retirement	149	5
Hobbies produce some income	172	6

[1] The percentages given for those who regularly pursue hobbies (above the short-ruled line) are based on the total retirees. The other percentages (below the short-ruled line) are based on the number who do pursue hobbies. The percentages below the line do not always add to 100 because a few respondents in each group did not answer all the subsidiary questions.

However, Table 20 shows that there is some increase in the degree of participation in hobbies among those retirees aged 65 to 68; 84 percent of these persons report engaging in some hobby, whereas the degree of participation is slightly lower among both younger and older retirees. Even among the oldest group, however, almost three out of four spend time with one or more hobbies.

Formal Education

In contrast with participation in sports and hobbies, relatively few of the retirees—fewer than one in five—have undertaken formal education in recent years (Table 21). Again in contrast with the activities discussed earlier, their current studies represent a fairly recent interest for a significant number of the retirees.

Arts and crafts, small engine maintenance, gardening and other "how-to-do-it" subjects are the ones most frequently mentioned, although the subjects cover a wide spectrum from the most academic to the immediately practical. Economics, political science, creative writing, literature, biology and history have been studied by retirees; so have courses in planning one's estate, in reducing one's taxes, and in preparing oneself to take the licensing examinations for real estate broker. Foreign languages might fall into either category. Some retirees may have studied them to gain the ability to read in another language, but undoubtedly some of the interest in foreign language stems from the extensive travel that occupies a considerable part of the time of many retired managers and professionals.

Only about two out of five retirees report that their interest in the subjects they have studied goes back many years. Eighteen percent became interested in their subjects in the years just before they retired, and double that number trace their interest only to the postretirement period. This, of course, is in sharp contrast to the patterns shown in relation to sports and hobbies.

Furthermore, less time is spent by the retirees at formal studies than is spent pursuing hobbies or sports. Very few who have engaged in formal study spend more than fifteen hours a week at it, and almost half of the retirees devote fewer than five hours to studies.

Colleges and universities, community colleges, vocational schools, and the adult education programs of public school systems are all used by these older students.

Age does not seem to be a factor in determining the degree of participation in formal study. Among the retirees, participation rates vary from 15 percent to 20 percent in no clear pattern.

Table 21: Formal Study by Retirees[1]

	Number	Percent
Have pursued formal courses of study	639	17%
Subjects		
Arts; crafts; "how-to-do-it" courses	209	33
Foreign languages	130	20
Social sciences	110	17
Real estate; brokerage laws and practice	94	15
Literature; creative writing	64	10
Religion	61	10
Estate planning; taxes	44	7
"Retirement living"	38	6
Where studied		
College or university, including extension	211	33
Pubic school, adult education program	175	27
Vocational school, public and private	88	14
Community college	87	14
Church or synagogue	50	8
Museum or conservatory	17	3
Time spent		
Under 5 hours per week	312	49
5 to 15 hours per week	260	41
16 to 30 hours per week	28	4
Over 30 hours per week	10	2
When interest developed		
Many years ago	274	43
In the years just before retirement	117	18
Since retirement	233	36

[1]The percentages given for those who have engaged in formal study (above the short-ruled line) are based on the total retirees. The other percentages (below the short-ruled line) are based on the number who have engaged in formal study. The percentages below the line do not always add to 100 because a few respondents among the retirees did not answer all the subsidiary questions.

Travel

While few of the retirees spend time at study, most spend some time traveling for pleasure and a considerable number devote several months to recreational travel (Table 22). Nine out of ten of the retirees have traveled about the United States, and about four out of ten have visited Canada or Mexico. Almost half have traveled overseas.

Table 22: Recreational Travel[1]

	Number	Percent
Travel for pleasure	3,106	85%
Where?		
Within the United States	2,772	89
Overseas	1,438	46
Canada or Mexico	1,303	42
Time spent		
Under 1 month annually	993	32
1 to 3 months annually	1,852	60
4 to 6 months annually	186	6
Over 6 months annually	19	1
When interest began		
Many years ago	2,561	82
In the years just before retirement	291	9
Since retirement	180	6

[1] The percentages given for those who travel for pleasure (above the short-ruled line) are based upon the total retirees. The other percentages (below the short-ruled line) are based upon the number who do travel for pleasure. The percentages below the line do not always add to 100 because a few respondents in each group did not answer all the subsidiary questions.

About a third of the group confine such trips to periods under one month annually, but about six out of ten spend one to three months annually traveling. Age has little effect upon the propensity to travel. Only in the oldest group of retirees is there a slight reduction—to 76 percent—in the percentage who travel annually for pleasure.

How Time Was Spent "Yesterday"

In terms of a number of common activities, the retirees resemble most middle-class people in their allocation of time. "Yesterday" most of them spent a little time reading the newspaper and a magazine or two, watching television, visiting friends (Chart 3). About four in ten of the retirees even spent some time loafing.

Watching television is the only activity (of those on the chart) that occupied three or more hours of the time of any considerable number of retirees. About a quarter spent more than three hours watching television, although for most of them four hours was the maximum. Visiting family or friends was also apt to take more than an hour or two, but fewer of the retirees visited family or friends "yesterday."

"Yesterday," of course, varied depending upon when the respondent completed the questionnaire; it was some day in the summer of 1976. And for many, "yesterday" was not a typical example of how they spend their time.

It was known from a field test of the questionnaire prior to the actual survey that many respondents would be concerned that "yesterday" was atypical. Therefore the questionnaire provided for an explanation of what was different about activities "yesterday." For some, "yesterday" had rain and so they could not work outside as they usually do; others spent all of "yesterday" working in the garden. Some say that "yesterday" was atypical because the children and grandchildren visited all day; for others, it was atypical because the grandchildren were sick and could not visit. "Yesterday" some had a committee meeting all day; others spent all day at home because it was Sunday.

Over a group as large as that in this study, however—3,679 retired managers and professionals—the reasons why "yesterday" was atypical tend to cancel out. While for any given person the pattern of activities reported on Chart 3 may not be typical, for the retirees in general the patterns shown represent a typical day. Indeed, it may well be close to the pattern of many middle-class people. If all the time allocations are added, these common activities, excluding loafing, take somewhat less than six hours of the day of retirees.

Chart 3: Time Spent by Retirees "Yesterday" at Various Common Activities

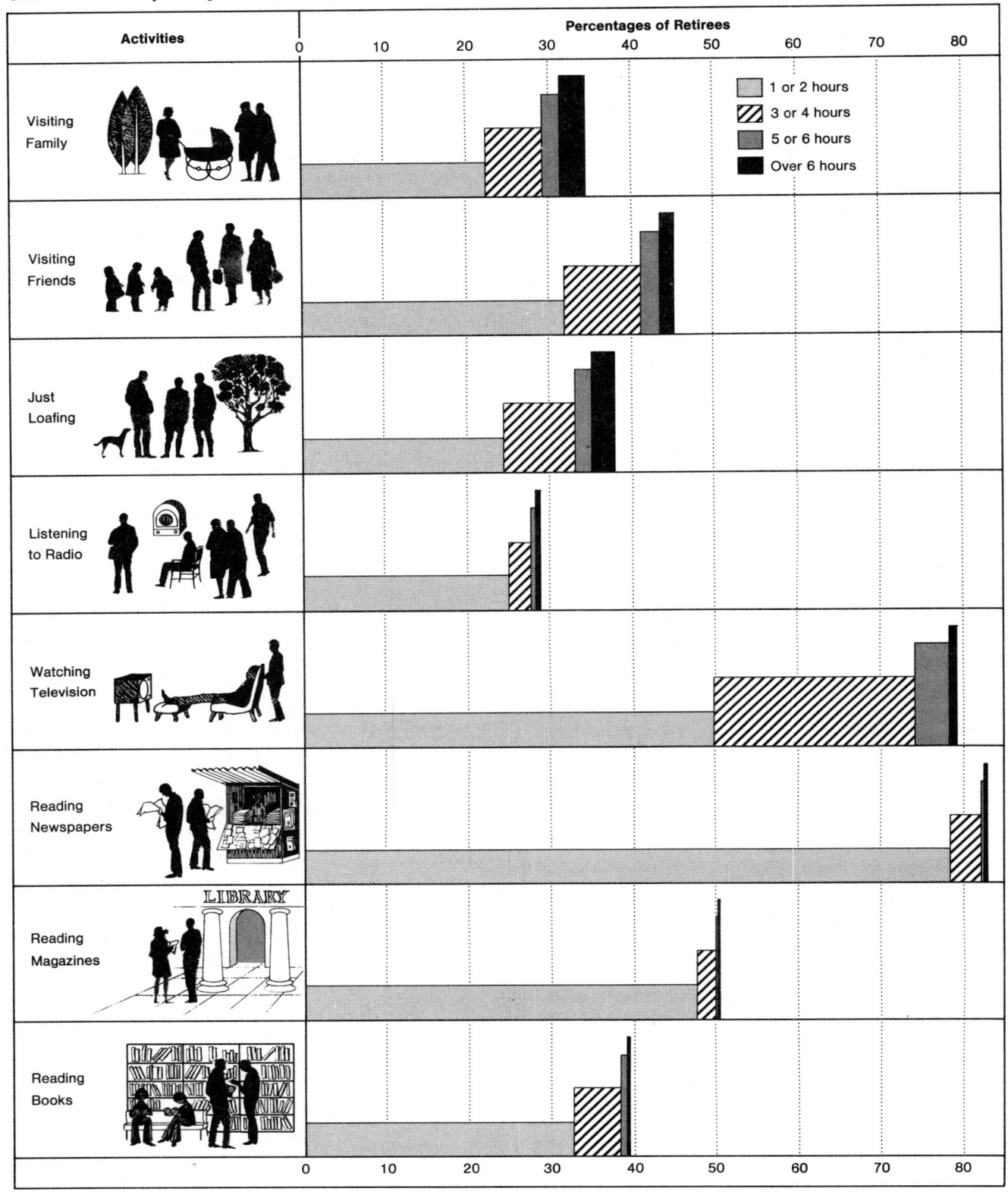

Activities	Percentages of Retirees
Visiting Family	
Visiting Friends	
Just Loafing	
Listening to Radio	
Watching Television	
Reading Newspapers	
Reading Magazines	
Reading Books	

Legend:
- 1 or 2 hours
- 3 or 4 hours
- 5 or 6 hours
- Over 6 hours

32   THE CONFERENCE BOARD

Chapter 5
The Quality of Life

THE RETIREES IN this study are remarkably satisfied with their lives. As mentioned in Chapter 1, 95 percent of the retirees add the statement ". . . and I like that" after categorizing themselves as completely retired, partially retired, or not retired at all. They report far more satisfaction than dissatisfaction with their paid work and volunteer activities. When asked what might improve the quality of their lives, many say simply: "I am happy as I am."

To gain additional information about how the respondents feel about their lives, they were asked to agree or disagree with eighteen statements about life and living that make up the "Life Satisfaction Index Z" developed by the sociologist, Dr. Robert Havinghurst. The Index had been used as part of the study for the National Council on the Aging mentioned earlier. The data from that study on the responses of the general population of the country aged 65 and over serve as a convenient reference point for comparing the answers given by the retirees. Table 23 presents that comparison. The shaded entries are those that are generally positive in tone.

About two-thirds agree with the statement: "As I grow older, things seem better than I thought they would be." Almost nine out of ten of the retirees (but only about three-quarters of the general public over 65) reject the idea: "This is the dreariest time of my life." The responses of the retirees on several items are significantly more positive than those of the general public.

On 14 of the 18 items, two-thirds or more of the retirees gave positive responses. The majority did not give positive responses on only two items—"My life could be happier than it is now" and "These are the best years of my life." However, there are many "Not Sure" responses on those items.

Nine in ten agree with the statement that: "Compared to other people my age, I make a good appearance"; almost no one disagrees. One man who did not answer this item added the marginal note: "I make a good appearance. I never compare myself with others."

A "Satisfaction Index" was computed for each of the respondents by scoring 2 for every positive response, 1 for every "Not Sure," and 0 for every negative answer, and summing the values. Thus, if someone chose the negative option in every case, the index would be zero; the highest possible index is 36.

The range of index scores for the retirees extends from a single very low 2 to many euphoric 36's. High scores predominate. The median is 30 and one-quarter have scores of 33 or above. Only one-quarter of the retirees have scores of 26 or below. The median for the older population at large is 26.

A comparison of the index scores with the ages of the retirees reveals a slight tendency for the older retirees to have lower scores. Only half of the individual items in the series show any relationship with age, however. The items on

Table 23: "Satisfaction with Life" of the Retirees and the Public Aged 65 and Over

Statements from the Havinghurst "Life Satisfaction Index Z"	Agree Retirees	Agree General Public	Disagree Retirees	Disagree General Public	Not Sure Retirees	Not Sure General Public
As I grow older, things seem better than I thought they would be.	66%	64%	15%	26%	19%	10%
I have gotten more of the breaks in life than most of the people I know.	71	63	11	27	18	10
This is the dreariest time of my life.	5	23	88	72	8	5
I am just as happy as when I was younger.	67	56	19	38	14	6
My life could be happier than it is now.	28	45	46	46	27	9
These are the best years of my life.	38	32 [a]	32	38 [a]	31	10 [a]
Most of the things I do are boring or monotonous.	5	14	89	82	6	4
I expect some interesting and pleasant things to happen to me in the future.	60	57	9	26	31	17
The things I do are as interesting to me as they ever were.	82	72	10	24	8	4
I feel old and somewhat tired.	16	46	72	50	12	4
As I look back on my life I am fairly well satisfied.	90	87	4	10	6	3
I would not change my past life even if I could.	51	62	25	29	24	9
Compared to other people my age, I make a good appearance.	91	83	1	6	8	11
I have made plans for things I'll be doing a month or a year from now.	71	53 [a]	20	43 [a]	9	6 [a]
When I think back over my life, I didn't get most of the important things I wanted.	11	32	75	61	14	7
Compared to other people, I get down in the dumps too often.	4	13	87	81	9	6
I've gotten pretty much what I expected out of life.	84	82	5	12	11	6
In spite of what some people say, the lot of the average man is getting worse, not better.	15	34	69	45	16	21

[a] These are the published data. The data for the public at large, aged 65 and over, are from The Myth and Reality of Aging in America, published by The National Council on the Aging, 1975, and were derived from a carefully drawn sample of the United States.

Note: Shaded figures are positive responses.

which older retirees tend to be somewhat more negative are:

- "I am just as happy as when I was younger."
- "These are the best years of my life."
- "I expect some interesting and pleasant things to happen to me in the future."
- "I feel old and somewhat tired."
- "I have made plans for things I'll be doing a month or a year from now."
- "When I think back over my life, I didn't get most of the important things I wanted."
- "In spite of what some people say, the lot of the average man is getting worse, not better."

On two items—"I would not change my past life even if I could" and "Compared to other people, I get down in the dumps too often"—the oldest retirees tend to be more positive than their juniors.

The Highly Satisfied and the Least

A comparison was made to determine, if possible, what distinguished those retirees who had scored in the upper quartile of the index from those who had scored in the lowest quartile. Most differences were slight on the factors examined.

As already mentioned, age is a factor. The median age of those with the lowest scores is 70 and of those with the highest it is 68, compared with a median age of 69 for all the retirees. The difference between the lowest and the highest, however appears to arise because of the greater number of persons below the age of 65 in the high-scoring group, not because of a greater number of older persons in the low-scoring group.

The educational levels of the high and low scorers do not differ from each other, or from the levels for the total retiree group. Similarly, the current after-tax income for the high and low scorers does not differ from that of all the retirees. However, current income as a percentage of the after-tax income earned in the last preretirement year is somewhat higher for both the high and low scorers than for the total retiree group. The current income of both high- and low-scoring groups is 61 to 70 percent of that earned in the last preretirement year; for the total retiree group the median is 51 to 60 percent.

Time spent watching television is considered by some to be an important factor affecting one's outlook on life. On average, the low scorers do spend somewhat more time in front of the tube than do the very satisfied—but the difference is slight. Fifty percent of both high and low scorers say that they spent one or two hours "yesterday" watching television. However, almost a third of the high scorers—but only about one in five of the low—did not watch it at all. Almost none of the very satisfied retirees watched for more than four hours; significantly more of the low scorers did.

The extra time for television for the low scorers may come because fewer of them are involved in work—paid or volunteer. About nine in ten of the high scorers, but only about two-thirds of the low scorers, engage in income-producing or volunteer work.

Health and general physical condition is the factor that most clearly distinguishes the two groups. Although about three-quarters of the relatively dissatisfied low scorers say that their health and physical condition is as good or better today than it was in the decade prior to retiring, nine in ten of the high scorers make this claim. A quarter of the low scorers—but only 10 percent of the high scorers—say that their health is worse today than it was before they retired.

"Satisfaction" or "Optimism"

The "Satisfaction Index" may be somewhat misleading as a clue to the satisfaction experienced by older persons. A number of retirees with index scores in the lowest quartile of the range answered another question—about how their retirement lives could be improved—by saying "I have nothing to suggest," and "I am happy as I am."

Positive responses were needed to get high index scores. A number of retirees obtained fairly low scores without giving any negative responses; they merely checked numerous "Not Sure's" and relatively few positive responses. In that sense, to be unsure of the positive option was in itself a negative response. Yet, as one marginal note says (alongside the item "I would not change my past life even if I could"): "Only a damned fool wouldn't change *anything* in his past life." He left the item blank, which was counted as "Not Sure" in computing the index.

Therefore, the index may not be tapping "satisfaction with life" but rather a generally optimistic and positive attitude toward life. The high scorers differ from the low not so much in the circumstances of their lives but in their reaction to them. The highly "satisfied" are certain in their positive choices; the retirees in the lowest quartile of the index distribution are, for the most part, unsure whether to choose the positive or the negative option for many items in Table 24.

In this regard, it may be significant that the largest proportion of highly "satisfied" retirees is found among those who are engaged in volunteer service to their local churches, which generally stress a positive outlook.

Improving the Quality of Retirement Life

When asked the question—"If you could have one realistic improvement in the quality of your retirement, what would it be?"—about a quarter of the retirees left the space blank, even among those who did make suggestions for improving the lives of other older persons. The blank space may be an answer similar to that of the 10 percent who wrote in the word "None." If so, about a third of these older persons are content. An additional 6 percent of the retirees underscored that message in the blank space:

- "I'm happy."
- "Perfectly content."
- "Quite happy now."
- "I'm happy as I am."
- "My wife would say 'Let's do more things together.' I'm pretty content."

About one in six of the retirees are concerned about money and inflation, as their various replies to the "one realistic improvement" question indicate:

- "Get rid of the ridiculous limit set by the social security system so that a person can supplement his sparse social security benefits."
- "Ability to cope with inflation."
- "Social security benefits that truly reflect the real inflation spiral."

"A more profitable stock market and a larger pension indexed for inflation."

- "Additional pension income: The cost of living has gone up so much and pensioners do not receive adjustments the way workers do."
- "Personally, I am happy, but like most retirees I am concerned with increased costs, inflation, taxes, government expenditures, and liberal socialistic antibusiness trends."

Concern about income and inflation is expressed as often by retirees in the higher income brackets of this study as by those in the lower. The erosion of what they have is what seems to bother most of them more than the absolute level of their income.

About one in eight of the retirees comment that life would be more enjoyable if they could travel more. The following comments are typical of their wishes:

- "More travel." (He now travels within the United States one to three months annually.)
- "Travel more." (He travels in the United States, Canada, Mexico and overseas for one to three months annually.)
- "Be able to afford more travel."
- "Have my wife's health improve so we could travel more."

A desire for improved health—for one's spouse or children as much as for oneself—is mentioned by about one in ten of the retirees:

- "Improvement in my wife's health; she has been paralyzed for several years."
- "Better physical condition—I have angina."

• "To play tennis, I stopped because of a coronary."
• "Good health for my wife."
• "Improvement in the health of one of my adult children."
• "Improved eyesight; cataracts limit some activities I used to enjoy, such as tennis and hunting."

(One does not know whether or not to classify under "health" the wish of one retiree: "To have more sex"; or that of another: "For a more active sex life.")

About one in five of the retirees mention friends and companionship as elements that would improve the quality of their retirement lives. Here are some typical replies:

• "More time to go visit friends."
• "More association with friends and more time to do so."
• "More opportunity for intelligent and informal conversation with other men" (from an older executive who is a full-time lawyer and a corporate director).
• "More communication from former employer."
• "More complete and frequent word in regard to former associates in my work during my employment with the only company I ever worked for."

Many of the comments cannot be categorized; these older persons are individuals and are expressing individual desires for "one realistic improvement":

• "Play better golf.
• "Be 40 years younger."
• "Have my wife happier in my retirement."
• "Introduce more flexibility into my calendar of duties."
• "Live in an area with more pleasant winter weather, which we will shortly be doing."
• "Quit smoking."
• "More education" (This is from an older executive, 75 years of age, who never completed high school.)

• "Closer and more geographically convenient association with a university."
• "Fish raising for profit in Oregon."
• "A horse ranch."
• "Sanity in our national government and social order."

Suggestions for Others like Oneself

Most of the same themes appear when the retirees respond to the question: "Based upon your knowledge of others your age with similar background, what single factor would do most to improve the quality of their retirement?" Adequate retirement income and protection against its erosion by inflation, as well as good health, companionship, travel and the enjoyment of family life are all mentioned. However, they are mentioned with decreased relative frequency because of the addition of three themes that are seldom mentioned in relationship to one's own life, but are given as advice: planning, purposeful activity, and—"meaningful" (or paid) employment.

A relative few mention early preparation for retirement: "Plan your retirement early in life," says one retiree. "Begin your planning at least five years in advance, preferably ten," says another. A few stress the value of corporate preretirement preparation programs and make suggestions for their content, such as this one: "The company should let people know about opportunities for paid and volunteer employment."

Another relatively small number stress an attitude toward retirement living when answering the question:

• "A more optimistic attitude."
• "Accept retirement and enjoy life; don't relate it to old age."
• "Discipline, in health habits and in concern for others."
• "Eliminate the thought that retirement classifies you as a recipient rather than as a contributor."
• "They should not let themselves retrogress nor live in the past."

The piece of advice on which there is the greatest agreement—mentioned by half of the retirees—is "Keep busy." For many, that imperative encompasses all there is to say.

- "Get going again."
- "Breadth and diversity of interests."
- "More activities."
- "Try to establish some hobbies before retiring."
- "Arts and crafts."
- "Do things that you did not have time to do before; do different things, like gardening instead of golf, janitor work instead of accounting."
- "Work at *something* to facilitate living in the present and future rather than in the past."

For many, however, merely keeping busy is not enough; the activity has to have a purpose:

- "Keep constructively active."
- "They need more meaningful, productive work to do."
- "They are a sad lot who pretend to like only leisure activities. Those who are employed are happier—and so are their wives."

The terms "meaningful" and "constructive," for certain of the retirees are equated with paid employment. Some of their comments are:

- "More business activity."
- "Continue employment beyond 65 if physically and mentally able."
- "Continue to be active in one's chosen professional field."
- "The good fortune to find work as satisfying as mine." (From the chairman of the board of a commercial bank—a "retiree").

In giving advice, a slightly larger number of the retirees see the "meaningful" nature of volunteer work:

- "Less time for golf and more for public affairs."
- "The times demand the input of concerned and capable citizens."
- "Become more involved with community activities."
- "An interest in some volunteer activity in which they can share their talents."
- "Keep busy on constructive community activities with one's peers and with persons of all ages."
- "Become involved with activities of a volunteer nature for community benefit, especially where younger people are participating."

"Working" and "Nonworking" Retirees Compared

Because of the stress laid by the retirees on the importance of keeping active, especially in meaningful and worthwhile pursuits, as being a means to a better quality of life, a comparison was made of a group of very active retirees with another, less active group. The "active" group were involved in income-producing work, volunteer work, or both, for at least half of a normal working schedule; many of these, particularly those engaged in paid work, were involved full time. The comparison group was not necessarily inactive but they had never engaged in either paid or volunteer work since they retired.

Whatever it is that the "Satisfaction with Life Index" measures, the "working retirees" show significantly more of it than do the "nonworking retirees." The former have a median index score of 31—higher than that for the retiree group as a whole. The "nonworking retirees" have a median score of 27, and the first and third quartile points are also lower than those of either the entire retiree sample or of the "working retiree" subgroup.

The difference may arise because the "working retirees" enjoy better health, at least as indicated by a comparison of the retirees' current physical condition with that enjoyed in the decade prior to retiring. About three-quarters of both the "working" and "nonworking" retirees say that their health is "about the same," as compared with only two-thirds of the total retiree sample. However, almost one in five of the "working retirees"—but only about one in twenty of the "nonworking retirees"—say that their health is "better now." Still, that means that about eight of ten "nonworking retirees," compared with about nine of ten "working retirees," are enjoying at least as good health as they did prior to retiring.

Age is probably not the factor that accounts for difference in "Life Satisfaction" between the two groups because the median age of the "working" and "nonworking" retirees is the same (69) as for the entire retiree sample. The "working retirees" do include slightly younger persons than do the "nonworking retirees," while the reverse is true for the older persons, but the differences are very small.

There is a difference in current income between the two groups. The median after-tax income of the "working retirees" is the same as for the total retiree group—between $20,000 and $25,000—while for the "nonworking retirees' the median lies between $15,000 and $20,000. As a percent of after-tax earnings in the last preretirement year, current income of the "working retirees" is higher—61 to 70 percent—compared with the 51 to 60 percent enjoyed by the "nonworking retirees," and by the total retiree sample.

In terms of former careers, the only striking differences are that former bankers are overrepresented in the "working" group and underrepresented in the "nonworking" group, and that former corporate officers (but not chief executives) are overrepresented among the "working retirees," while former middle managers are overrepresented among the "nonworking retirees."

The educational level of the "nonworking retirees" is slightly lower than that of either the total retiree sample or the "working retirees." The average "nonworking retiree" has had some college but did not complete it, while the average retiree and "working retiree" is a college graduate.

A striking difference shows up in terms of television viewing. About half of all three comparison groups watched television for an hour or two "yesterday." But about four in ten of the "working retirees" did not watch it at all; most of the remaining "working retirees" watched between three and four hours of television and many of them seemed to apologize for the fact by adding the note that "It was Sunday." In contrast, only about one in ten of the "nonworking retirees" did not watch at all; almost a third sat in front of the tube for three to four hours; and about 10 percent spent even more time watching television "yesterday."

What seems to differentiate the "working from the "nonworking" retirees, then, is simply that the former are more active. For whatever reason—greater opportunities, as the preponderance of former corporate officers might suggest; greater awareness of what is going on in a community, which might be true of former bankers; somewhat better health—the "working retirees" have followed the advice that retirees and other executives give for having contented older years: They have kept busy at something they think is worthwhile.

THE QUALITY OF LIFE

Appendix

About the Retirees

In order to obtain information about the current activities of former managers and professional employees in major U.S. companies, The Conference Board sought the cooperation of the 1,300 firms in the various lists published by *Fortune* magazine. These include the nation's largest manufacturers, banks, insurance firms, utilities, wholesale and retail merchandising companies, transportation firms, and communications companies.

Two hundred and thirty-four companies agreed to assist by selecting for the survey sample up to 30 persons who had retired within the previous 15 years and who, at the time of retirement, had occupied positions at middle management or higher. A salary criterion was used to define the lower level of "middle management": different figures were used for manufacturing and nonmanufacturing firms and a criterion salary was set for each of the 15 years that reflected the average middle-management salary in that industry in the given year.

Almost one-third of the firms (76) sent the names and addresses of retirees to The Conference Board on the understanding that the lists would be destroyed as soon as the survey envelopes were addressed. The names of 1,984 retirees were obtained in that way. The remaining firms refused to divulge the names of their retirees but agreed to address survey envelopes that were sent to them in bulk. A total of 4,450 questionnaire packets were sent to these firms.

All mailings included a business-reply envelope addressed to the Board. Thus the retirees could be assured of anonymity; the companies for which they had worked would never see their replies and The Conference Board had no list of the persons to whom the questionnaire had been sent. Of course, the name and address of the respondent was not asked for on the questionnaire.

A total of 3,820 replies were received, 3,679 of them in time to be put into the computer for analysis. Replies continued to come in until a year after the original mailing in the summer of 1976; the retirees seemed eager to respond.

It is possible only to estimate the percentage response because of the way the questionnaire was distributed. If all 6,434 questionnaires sent by the Board, either directly to retirees or to companies, had in fact been mailed, the response rate would be 59 percent—very high for a mail survey. However, it is known that many firms overestimated the number of persons they would find who met the selection criteria. If only 80 percent of the forms sent in bulk to companies were remailed by them to retirees, the response rate would be an extremely high 69 percent. Based upon comments from a few cooperating firms, it is assumed that this is a close approximation of the actual rate of response.

The Former Work of the Retirees

The industries in which the retirees formerly worked are shown in Table 24. In their former positions, 21 percent of the retirees were

Table 24: Industries in which Retirees Formerly Worked[1]

	Number	Percent
Manufacturing, durable goods	1,181	33%
Manufacturing, nondurable goods	794	22
Transportation	196	5
Utilities	305	8
Wholesale and retail trade	196	5
Insurance	271	7
Banking and finance	464	13
Communications	35	1
Mining, extractive	105	3
Other	73	2
Total	3,620	

[1] Percentages do not add to 100 because of rounding.

primarily professionals, making their chief contribution through their own specialized knowledge and skill, although they may have had some managerial responsibilities (Table 25). The remaining 79 percent of the retirees were primarily managers. Of these, 9 percent were formerly the chief executive officers of their firms, 29 percent were corporate officers (other than CEO's), and 62 percent worked at middle-management levels.

"General administration" is the function in which 36 percent of the retirees say they were working at the time they retired (Table 26). Many—but not all—of these individuals were formerly chief executives and other corporate

Table 25: Type of Former Position[1]

Former Work	Number	Percent
Primarily managerial	2,835	79%
Primarily professional	769	21
Total	3,604	100
Of those whose positions were primarily managerial:		
Chief Executive Officer	253	9
Other Corporate Officer	814	29
Middle Manager	1,731	62
Total	2,798	100

[1] The percentages at the top of the table are based on the total of those answering that question. The percentages for the managerial level are based on those answering the question concerning level. Not all the retirees who said that their former positions were primarily managerial gave the level of their postions.

Table 26: Former Functional Area of Management

	Number	Percent
General administration	1,296	36%
Production or engineering (in manufacturing)	371	10
Operations (in nonmanufacturing)	177	5
Research and development	160	4
Sales, including sales management	472	13
Other marketing	79	2
Finance	386	11
Legal	84	2
Personnel	168	5
Public relations	58	2
Purchasing	93	3
Distribution	33	1
Internal consulting	38	1
Other	189	5
Total	3,604	100

officers. Included, however, are some retirees who rank themselves as having been in middle management but who say that their responsibilities were corporatewide. Some of the officers on the other hand, place themselves in a functional area such as production or sales. Even a few former chief executives say that they were primarily involved in sales, rather than general administration.

Finally, most of the retirees had long tenure with one, or only a few, companies. More than two-thirds had worked for 31 years or more for the firm from which they retired. A mere 2 percent had spent ten years or fewer with the company. Only 13 percent of the retirees had worked for five or more companies or other organizations during their preretirement careers, while 29 percent had worked for only one organization for their entire careers (Chart 4). The phrase "the only company I ever worked for..." appears frequently in the responses of the retirees—sometimes proudly, sometimes as a poignant comment.

Current Income

The median income of the retirees, after taxes, is $20,600. This is *family* income and includes the income of a spouse if the retiree is married, as most of them are. However, it does

APPENDIX 41

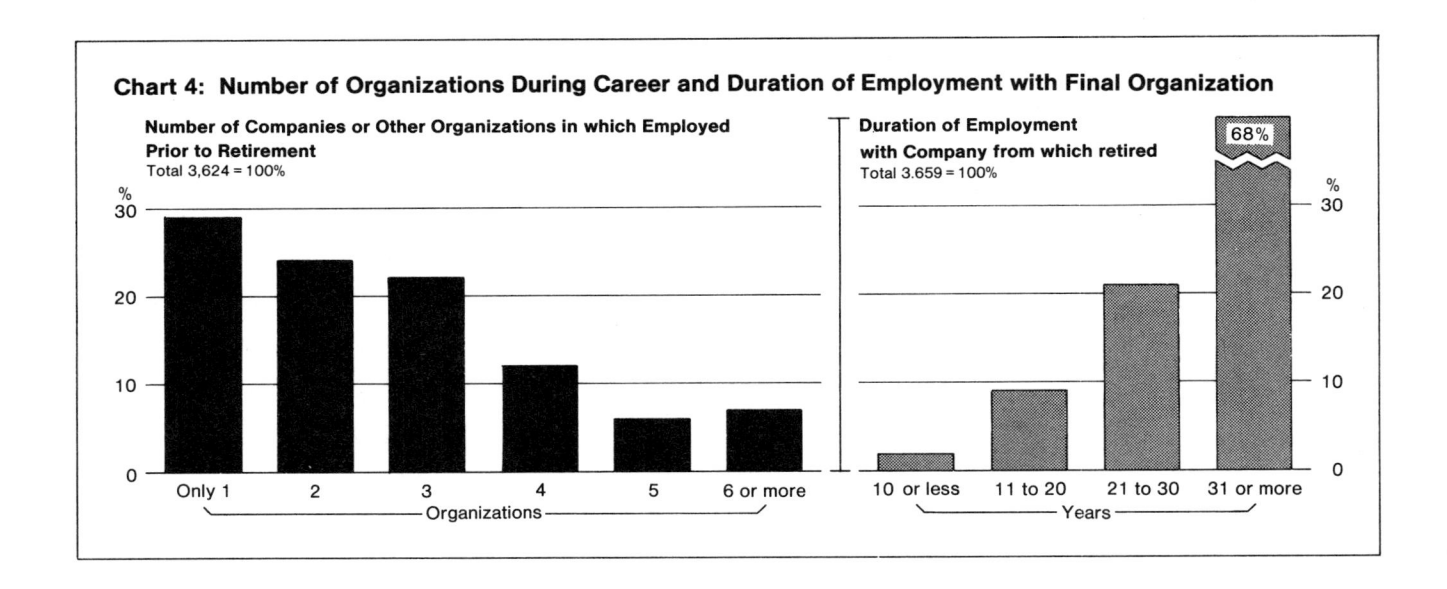

Chart 4: Number of Organizations During Career and Duration of Employment with Final Organization

not include the income of any other household members, even if they are relatives. The distribution of annual family income after taxes, for the retirees is given in Table 27.

Seventeen of the retirees have incomes of under $4,000; they are fewer than one-half of one percent of the retiree group. In contrast, 171 of the retirees (5 percent) have incomes, after taxes, of $60,000 or more.

About one in five of the retirees now has an annual income that is only 40 percent or less of preretirement after-tax earnings. But about an equal number have incomes today that are at least 81 percent of preretirement incomes. The average retiree has a current income that is about half of his preretirement income.

The most important source of income for about half the retirees is a company pension; 95 percent list this source as being among the first three sources in importance in contributing to current spendable funds (Table 28). Investment income and interest on savings accounts is the next most important source; for 88 percent of the retirees it is among the three most important sources, and for a third of them it is the prime source of funds.

In spite of the number of retirees who are engaged in income-producing work, it produces

Table 27: Annual Family Income After Taxes[1]

	Number	Percent
Under $4,000	17	a
$4,000 to $6,999	51	1
$7,000 to $9,999	251	7
$10,000 to $14,999	690	19
$15,000 to $19,999	722	20
$20,000 to $24,999	562	16
$25,000 to $29,999	385	11
$30,000 to $34,999	271	8
$35,000 to $39,999	177	5
$40,000 to $49,999	214	6
$50,000 to $59,999	94	3
$60,000 and over	171	5
Total	3,605	
Median:	$20,600	

As a percent of preretirement after tax income

	Number	Percent
20 percent or less	139	4
21 to 30 percent	193	6
31 to 40 percent	315	9
41 to 50 percent	602	17
51 to 60 percent	571	16
61 to 70 percent	498	14
71 to 80 percent	489	14
81 to 90 percent	291	8
91 percent or more	375	11
Total	3,473	

[a]Less than one-half of one percent.
[1]Percentages do not add to 100 because of rounding.

Table 28: Sources of Current Spendable Funds[1]

	Relative Importance of the Source							
	Most Important Source		Second Most Important Source		Third Most Important Source		Among First Three in Importance	
Sources of Current Spendable Funds:	Number	Percent	Number	Percent	Number	Percent	Number	Percent
Company pension	1,839	50%	1,335	37%	287	8%	3,461	95%
Investment income and interest on savings	1,248	34	1,017	28	944	26	3,209	88
Social Security	208	6	902	25	1,582	43	2,692	74
Salary from paid work	240	7	147	4	200	5	587	16
Profits from business or fees from practice	51	1	70	2	95	3	216	6
Withdrawal from savings or sale of securities	6	a	41	1	83	2	130	4
Personally purchased annuities	10	a	34	1	59	2	103	3
Veteran's pension or other government pension	5	a	26	1	34	1	65	2
Other[2]	47	1	45	1	78	2	170	5

[1] Percentages are based upon the 3,650 retirees who resonded to any part of this question. They may not add to 100 percent because of rounding.
[2] This was usually said to be deferred compensation from former company.
[a] Less than one-half of one percent.

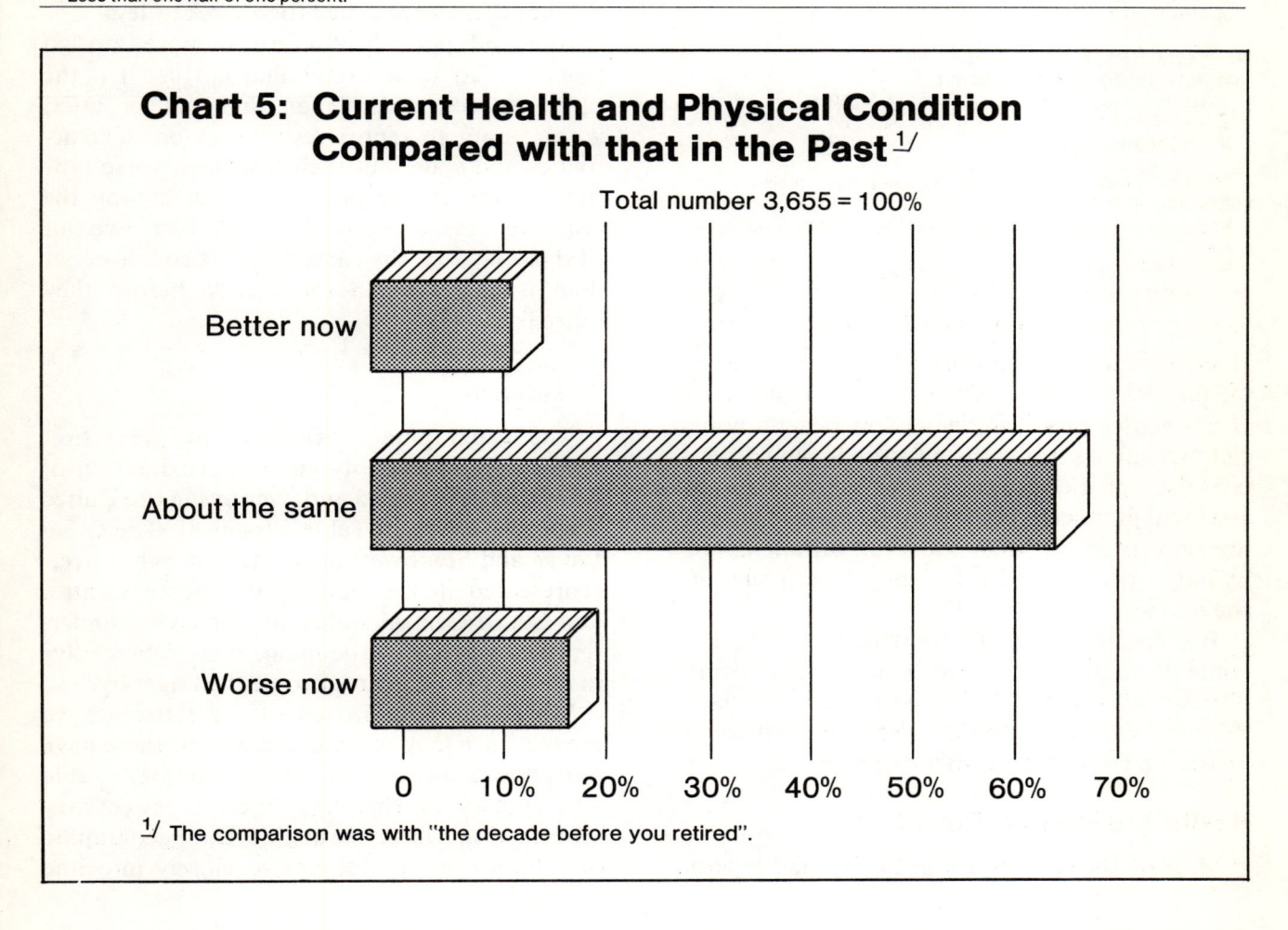

Chart 5: Current Health and Physical Condition Compared with that in the Past [1/]

Total number 3,655 = 100%

- Better now: ~17%
- About the same: ~67%
- Worse now: ~16%

[1/] The comparison was with "the decade before you retired".

APPENDIX 43

Table 29: Physical Condition during Three Months Prior to Survey[1]

	Number	Percent
Activities Restricted due to Physical Condition		
Activities restricted	669	18%[a]
Activities not restricted	2,983	81
Duration of Restriction		
Week or less	90	13[b]
About two weeks	95	14
About a month	106	16
About two months	126	19
About three months	239	36
Bed Confinement during Prior Three Months		
Confined to bed	309	8[a]
Not confined to bed	3,340	91
Duration of Confinement		
Week or less	167	54[b]
About two weeks	87	28
About a month	38	12
About two months	12	4
About three months	2	1
Normality of Physical Condition during Prior Three-Month Period		
Typical	3,266	89[a]
Better than usual	84	2
Worse than usual	297	8

[1] Percentages do not add to 100 because a few retirees did not answer appropriate items.

[a] These percentages are based on the total 3,679 retirees in the survey.

[b] These percentages are based upon the 669 retirees reporting activity restriction or the 309 reporting confinement to bed.

significant income for only 22 percent of them. Of the retirees, 16 percent list "Salary or wages from income-producing work" as being among the first three sources of their funds, and 6 percent list "profits or fees from business or professional practice." However, those two sources are said to be *the* single most important source by only 7 percent and 1 percent, respectively, of the retirees.

The former company contributes to the income of some of the retirees in another form: Almost all of the 5 percent who checked "Other" explained that this was deferred compensation from their former employer.

Health and Physical Condition

Most of the retirees are in fairly good health and physical condition. Two-thirds say that their condition today is about the same as it was a number of years ago (Chart 5). Indeed, 14 percent of the retirees say that their health is better now than it was in the past.

Of course, their health might not have been very good at some time in the past. That may have been the reason for retiring. Therefore, they were asked about any restrictions they had had to place upon their activities "in the last three months" because of health or physical conditions, and whether or not they had been confined to bed during that period.

Fewer than one in five had to restrict any planned activities for health reasons (Table 29). Those who did, however, faced such restrictions for two months or more of the period. On the other hand, relatively few were confined to bed during the period, only about 10 percent, and most of them were in bed for a week or less.

Age and poor health are supposed to go together. To some extent that is true; it is the older retirees, rather than the younger ones, who are apt to report restrictions on their activities and state that their health is worse now than it was in the past. But even among the oldest retirees, those aged 77 and older, two out of three say that their health is as good or better than it had been in the decade before they retired.

Residence

The geographic distribution of the retiree sample is a reasonably good approximation of where people aged 65 and over live in the United States, as shown in Table 1 (page 3). The Great Lakes and Southwest areas are somewhat overrepresented in the sample, the North Central and South Central states are somewhat underrepresented. But in the main, these retirees live in the areas where most people their ages live.

More than four in ten of the retirees have moved since they retired, and half of these have moved to another section of the country (Table 30). It may be that it is these cross-country moves that have brought the geographic distribution of the retirees so closely into line

Table 30: Residential Movement Since Retirement[1]

	Number	Percent
Change of residence since retirement	1,582	43%[a]
No change of residence since retirement	2,077	56
Type of Move		
A new home within same community	300	19[b]
A different community within the same region of the United States	486	31
A different region of the United States	753	48
Out of the United States	10	1
Return to the United States	17	1
Year regularly divided between two regions	1,464	40[a]
Year not divided between two regions	2,154	59

[1] Percentages may not add to 100 because a few retirees did not answer appropriate items.

[a] These percentages are based on the total 3,679 retirees in the survey.

[b] These percentages are based on the 1,582 retirees who have changed residence.

Table 31: Urban or Rural Residence[1]

	Number	Percent
Live within city limits[2]	1,464	40%
Live in other areas	2,154	59
City Population		
50,000 to 100,000	525	37
100,001 to 500,000	433	30
500,001 to 1,000,000	250	18
Over 1,000,000	216	15
Total	1,424	100
Areas other than a City		
A suburb on the edge of a city	1,011	50
A town or village in a rural area	676	33
A rural area not in a town or village	281	14
A farm in a rural area	58	3
Total	2,026	100
Distance from Nearest City		
5 miles or less	415	19
6 to 10 miles	338	16
11 to 15 miles	258	12
16 to 20 miles	234	11
21 to 25 miles	152	7
26 miles or more	732	34
Total	2,129	100[a]
Population of Nearest City		
50,000 to 100,000	765	36
100,001 to 500,000	642	31
500,001 to 1,000,000	341	16
Over 1,000,000	353	17
Total	2,101	100

[1] See text for discussion of discrepancies in this table.

[2] Defined on questionnaire as "within limits of a city of at least 50,000."

[a] These percentages do not add to 100 due to rounding.

with that of the general population of the U.S. over 65.

Most of the retirees, however, have not moved to new regions of the country. In fact, 57 percent have not moved at all and, of those who have, 40 percent have stayed in the same region, merely moving into a new home in the same or in a nearby community.

One percent of the retirees have moved out of the United States to settle elsewhere. Numerically they have been replaced by 1 percent who have moved back to the country from prior residence abroad.

It would appear from Table 31 that most of the retirees live in or near cities. However, there are a number of discrepancies in the figures that make interpretation of the table difficult. For one thing, an unusually large proportion of the retirees (6 percent) did not answer some part of the series of questions from which the table is derived. It is possible that some felt a concern that they might identify themselves by giving too much information about where they live, even though the categories were deliberately made broad enough so that such identification would be impossible.

Some who say that they live in a city do not give its population; some who say that they do not live in a city do not indicate what type of area they do live in. On the other hand, more people give information about how far away the nearest city is, and what its population is, than say that they live outside cities.

Because The Conference Board took pains *not* to know the names and addresses of the respondents to the survey, it has no way to resolve the discrepancies in Table 31. However, it is probable that the figures given there are at least a fairly good approximation of the residential patterns of retired managers in this country.